GRANDPARENTS ARE FOREVER

Carolyn Gutowski

PAULIST PRESS
New York/Mahwah, N.J.

Library of Congress Cataloging-in-Publication Data

Gutowski, Carolyn.
    Grandparents are forever / Carolyn Gutowski.
      p.   cm.
    Includes bibliographical references.
    ISBN 0-8091-3471-3 (pbk.)
    1. Grandparent and child. 2. Grandparenting—Religious aspects—
Christianity. I. Title.
HQ759.9.G88   1994
306.874′5—dc20   94-968
                                               CIP

Published by Paulist Press
997 Macarthur Boulevard
Mahwah, New Jersey 07430

Printed and bound in the
United States of America

TABLE OF CONTENTS

PREFACE

Grateful memories of my own grandparents and of my parents as grandparents have led me to appreciate personally how important and even necessary grandparents are for the well-being of the family, indeed of the whole younger generation. To apprise grandparents of their continuing vocation and to give them concrete insights into its realization has been my mission in writing a book that blends the theoretical and the practical.

My own professional interest in this area goes back to 1983 and a groundbreaking conference on Grandparents and Family Connections, the first such national scholarly conference on this key topic. Held at the Wingspread Conference Center in Racine, Wisconsin, it was convened by the National Institute for the Family and the William Petschek National Jewish Family Center of the American Jewish Committee. The consensus emerged that the message must move from the academics to the grandparents themselves. In my own efforts, through lectures and workshops, to bring this message to those actually grandparenting, I owe much to the inspiring participants at the first conference, especially Vern L. Bengtson, David L. Gutmann, Arthur Kornhaber, Joan F. Robertson, and Harlan J. Wechsler.

Many people have contributed to this book. Most of them have been active grandparents whose lives of love and service have illustrated the richness and joys of their intergenerational call. From them I have learned the true potentialities of grandparents.

In an additional way, two others have helped me greatly. Dr. Donald Conroy insightfully deepened my knowledge of two topics of fundamental importance to the human family, regenerative aging and environmental awareness. Especially, however, I wish to acknowledge the wisdom and scholarly precision of Dr. David Granfield, who has gently guided and encouraged me during the writing of this book. All those I have mentioned and many others have earned my heartfelt gratitude for helping me project my cherished vision that the life-giving influence of grandparents endures beyond our imagining.

DEDICATION

For my Father and Mother,
Anthony and Jean,
whose loving wisdom
has been for me
the perfect model of regenerative
grandparenting

INTRODUCTION

A grandparent's legacy may last for ages. When this influence reflects the wisdom and love of the Creator, it becomes an enduring wellspring of goodness that flows into the future. The title of this book reflects the exhilarating expectation that grandparents are indeed forever.

The Psalmist sang of this spiritual longevity: "O God, you have taught me from my youth until now; I declare your wonders. Yea, even to old age and gray hairs, do not forsake me, O God; so that I may tell of your mighty arm to the generations, to all that are to come" (Ps 71:17–18). Like the rays of the sun, unconditional love and shared wisdom communicate an abiding heritage to grandchildren, a heritage that can be handed down from generation to generation.

Grandparents, living reminders of all one's ancestors, prepare their descendants to take up the task of building a better world. As links to the past and guides to the future, they provide insights based on years of experience that can shed light on the problems facing each new generation.

Robert Mueller, former United Nations Assistant Secretary General, observed that as we age we become more spirit than body. We all need to attune ourselves to the spiritual meaning of life. For most people, the major source of this development is their own family, their children, and their grandchildren.

By relating to grandchildren, grandparents themselves become further transformed. Interacting in loving ways, they integrate their own talents and spiritual energies through a

1

renewed sense of values and the discovery of a clearer mission for their remaining years. This expanded horizon brings their maturity to fulfillment through a wholehearted giving which reconstitutes their whole life. Instead of settling back as passive spectators, they rejoice as active participants. Indeed, grandchildren afford them a second chance at the gold ring.

This book, *Grandparents Are Forever*, enables men and women to reclaim their powers through regenerative grandparenting. By following a fivefold pattern, grandparents are able to build warm and productive relationships. Grandparents discover new and creative ways to enhance their grandchildren's lives as well as their own. In addition to meeting the immediate needs of grandchildren, grandparents are able to enrich and invigorate the total family system and renew the wider world.

Contemporary grandparents and their adult children can benefit from this timely book. The full scope is even wider: family educators, social workers, family counselors, pastoral ministers, intergenerational program developers, and older persons who relate to members of the younger generation—in short, people of any age who appreciate the legacy of their own grandparents and who consider all grandparents to be agents of change. Let us next look at the five roles for regenerative grandparents.

Chapter 1 examines the role of grandparents as *Nurturers*. Grandparents develop emotional bonds between themselves and their grandchildren by expressions of love, unconditional but prudent. This love is manifested in practice by attention, concern, and care. By so acting, grandparents fashion the heart of the child to become sensitive and caring toward others and all God's creation. Often they intervene in times of family stress—divorce, addiction, illness, death—to offer assistance to their grandchildren and to their own adult children. They devote themselves to building up the spirit of the grandchild, a task that renews their own spirit as well.

Chapter 2 focuses on grandparents as *Family Historians*—living ancestors who bridge the gap between the past and the present. They reconstruct from their treasure chest of memories stories that communicate a sense of family and cultural history. They make the past come alive and take on meaning. Children learn to situate themselves in the story of humankind. They find their roots and a new sense of dignity and responsibility.

Chapter 3 looks to grandparents as *Mentors*, who help to both teach life's skills for survival, renewal, and enhancement. Grandparents have acquired much practical know-how which, owing to economic security and relative freedom, they can easily pass on to young people. They possess flexibility and effectiveness derived from the challenge of having had to adapt to life's many changes. In reviving all but forgotten talents, grandparents begin to appreciate their own competence and their joyous opportunity to share these skills through teaching.

Chapter 4 examines the need for grandparents as *Models of Aging*. The young gain a sound perspective about the future by seeing their own flesh and blood grow old—gracefully and fruitfully. Grandparents can communicate a sense of inner peace during the final decades of life, if they themselves are able to adapt positively to these inevitable changes with hope and with joy. Margaret Mead noted that contemporary grandparents have lived through more changes in the last hundred years than any other generation. They can manifest abundantly how to meet life's challenges and to flourish, despite adverse odds.

Chapter 5 views grandparents as *Sages*. Grandparents, having successfully learned much in a long life, can find great satisfaction in sharing their hard-earned wisdom. As part of the "wisdom generation," to use psychologist Erik Erickson's felicitous term, they have learned to savor the balance of meanings and values that constitute a truly good life. In becoming a "wise person" for their grandchildren, they help to enlighten the child and to smooth its difficult road to maturity.

To conclude, this book has an urgent message for all concerned with family life and society. Now is the time to help them reclaim their destined role as "the elders of the tribe," so that they may share with their grandchildren a life seasoned by suffering, strengthened by love, and brightened by wisdom. By being Nurturers, Family Historians, Mentors, Models of Aging, and Sages, they fashion in their grandchildren the positive insights, attitudes and values that direct them on their journey through life. Grandparents thus instill in their loved ones a living legacy that will show for generations that grandparents are forever.

1

GRANDPARENTS AS *NURTURERS:* FASHIONING THE HEART

When parents have a child, they worry about the effect on their growing offspring of the rest of the world, a world with good and evil in it. When a couple adopts a child, they have an added concern, whether generating or parenting will prove the more decisive influence, whether the natural parents or the adoptive parents will more strongly determine the child's future.

Of course, both heredity and environment are necessary. It is not a question of nature *or* nurture, but nature *and* nurture. Every living being needs to be generated. But unlike tadpoles or young chicks, humans also need special nurturing, if they are fully to actualize their innate potential.

Defining the term nurture shows its importance and scope. To nurture means to feed, to rear, to foster, to cherish. Grandparents have produced and nurtured children who in turn produce and nurture their own children. The process continues generation after generation. All persons, even the elderly, have a need to be nourished, fostered, and cherished; everyone is nurtured so that they continue to grow in wisdom and love. For young people, the need is more pressing. And grandparents supply a natural safety net, a second ring of protection to guarantee this nurturing requirement.

The heart of nurturing is love. Each of us is born to love. To love is to become fully human. Indeed the call to love is a profound undertaking that holds great power and promise both for the one who is loved and the one who loves. Love has a magical quality—it preserves, it enables, and it transforms.

Without love our lives shrivel up. For example, infants deprived of loving human interaction often die. Satisfying only physical needs is not enough for the child's continuing physical and mental development. As far back as 1915, Dr. Henry Chapin reported, in a study of ten institutions for infants in the United States where every child under two years of age died, that the major factor was little or no personal contact and interaction. Other reports illustrating the surprising effects of this lack of nurturing in the lives of children indicate a relationship between the amount of physical contact and the nurturing a child receives and the development of perception, imitative ability, memory, intelligence, and personality. Children deprived of nurturing showed a significant drop in their intelligence rating.[1]

We cannot love without first being loved. Initially, we come to know the message of love through nurturing. The love in nurturing makes it a God-like act. Indeed, the human need for love has its roots in the divine, for "God is love, and he who abides in love abides in God and God in him" (I Jn 4:8). But even here the relationship is primarily a nurturing one on God's part, "because he has first loved us" (I Jn 4:10). As children of a loving Father, we must carry on this tradition of nurturing: "If God so loved us, we ought also to love one another" (I Jn 4:11). These words proclaim the great mission to which grandparents are called.

The Emotional Barriers

How ironic it is that Jean-Jacques Rousseau (1712-1778), who made the intellectual world aware of childhood, utterly refused his duty to nurture his own five children and secretly sent them as infants to a public orphanage and to almost certain death. "Two-thirds of the babies died in their first year. An average of fourteen out of every hundred survived to the age of seven."[2] Yet even in the twentieth century there were in Europe more statues of this French philosopher than of anyone else. His theories on politics and education were world-renowned. Their underlying perspective was that the state should form the minds of all children and adults alike. Such a public takeover by the state as primary nurturer would be monstrous. As Louis Sullivan, former Secretary of Health and Human Services, said in another context: "What we would have is a combination of the compassion of the IRS and the efficiency of the post office."[3]

Tragically, children who survive a lack of nurturing often grow up incapable of nurturing others. Rousseau's mother died when he was a mere infant. He had no sisters, just one brother seven years older. His father was brutal. His father and foster mother died when Jean-Jacques was still young. No doubt he never had the nurturing he needed. Certainly, he never gave the nurturing he should have. Deprivation begets deprivation.

The well-known educator and popular psychologist, Leo Buscaglia, describes his early experience: "My mother and father were my best teachers of love, because they never taught me, they showed me." Many of the emotionally wounded cannot treat their own children lovingly. Even as grandparents this coldness may continue. But grandparents as grandparents have a second chance—without the burden of full responsibility. Rousseau, however, had effectively killed his chances. None of his children lived long enough to give him grandchildren.

Most grandparents find it easy to nurture their grandchildren. That is not true of all of them. One grandmother, whom I recall meeting on a flight to Los Angeles, had a somewhat different type of problem but one which inhibited her in relating to her grandchildren. Looking self-assured and intelligent, she was dressed conservatively with simple but expensive jewelry. The small talk led to a question about grandchildren. She surprised me by saying that she had eighteen of them. But she did so with just a slight shrug—no smile.

"Do you see them often?" I asked. "Only on some holidays," she said, "and on occasional birthdays. I don't want to interfere." She explained that she owned a small florist shop and valued independence. Her expression then became pensive, even worried. "Here I am, a little over sixty, and I have never felt that I was any use to them at all." After a pause, she added: "Perhaps it is because I never had any grandparents. I never knew them, that is." Then another long pause, "But I can remember, when I was a child, envying my classmates when they spoke of their grandmother and grandfather. I felt cheated."

I decided to challenge her squarely: "Aren't you cheating your own grandchildren—and yourself?" Her response was a nervous laugh followed by a pensive smile. "Maybe I have been. I ought to think about it." We left the plane moments later, but I noticed a softness in her face that was not there when she first sat down beside me.

The Breakthrough

Grandchildren need grandparents, but some grandparents are not aware of it. Some grandparents take longer than others to discover this because they are too preoccupied with their own lives and life-styles, because they are simply uninformed, or because they have a fear of interfering or imposing. Many times the best one to break down the barriers is the grandchild. All the grandparents need to do is open their hearts and pay attention.

Several years ago a friend of mine, a successful salesman, stopped by my office for a short visit. Dennis, a father of six young adult daughters, became a grandfather in his late forties. As we chatted the conversation turned to his daughters and then to his grandchildren.

"I see them every once in a while," he responded to my inquiry. "But I have had it all, just raising my own children. Now I only want some peace and quiet. Seeing them for birthdays and holidays is enough for me."

The conversation ended on this disheartening note since

Dennis had to rush off to one of his appointments with a client. Because our meetings were so infrequent, we never picked up on that particular topic of conversation. Although uneasy about his failure to make more of an effort to see his grandchildren and his lack of awareness of their need for him in their lives, I sensed that this was not the time to pursue the matter further.

Several years passed after that conversation and the topic had never come up again. Then one spring day Dennis came by the office. From his lively tone, I knew he was anxious to share something important. Dennis was quick to begin.

"Last week my daughter telephoned Fern (his wife) and me to ask us to watch our seven year old grandson, Daniel, on the following Saturday. She had some pressing needs to tend to and was at a loss for a babysitter. We agreed to it."

"When Saturday arrived my daughter dropped off Daniel. I had to get a haircut and run some errands, so I thought I would take him along, s ɔ that Fern could get her ironing done without interruption."

"We were soon on our way." As the two of us walked, I noticed that my grandson was wearing a thin little jacket, though it was an especially cold winter day. "Don't you have anything warmer than that?" I asked.

"No, Grandpa. This is all I brought with me."

"That won't do," I told him. "We have to do something about that. So I took him to a store and bought him a warm coat, a blue one. He picked out the color."

"Next," I said, "I have to get a haircut. It looks like you could use one, too, Daniel. Let's both get one." But when we got close to the unisex haircuttery, Daniel noticed that women were cutting hair. As we were ready to walk through the door, Daniel balked, `I'm not going to let a girl cut my hair, Grandpa.'"

"I still have to get mine cut, Daniel," I said. After my hair had been cut I encouraged him to try it. "Well, okay," he said at last. Seeing me pass the test, and liking the results, challenged him to do the same. "In a short time a smiling little boy with a clean cut alighted from the chair."

"That wasn't so bad, Grandpa," he said.

"Finally, I mentioned to Daniel that before we return home, we should buy a bouquet of flowers for his mom. As we left the floral shop and started walking toward the car, Daniel, holding tightly the bouquet of white daisies, looked up at me and said, `Grandpa, I like you. You know so much. You're even smarter than my Dad.'"

"Only later that night did I recall a similar experience when my own uncle—I think he must have been about my age at the time—bought me a new jacket when I was a young boy about Daniel's age."

As Dennis ended his story I could sense the change that had occurred in the relationship between his grandson and himself in the two intervening years. These minor events had unleashed in him the love that all along was waiting to be enkindled. His feelings were a surprise to himself. He had broken through to the tender joys of grandparenting. He had suddenly discovered what most grandparents know instinctively—how important a grandparent can be to a grandchild and how strongly a grandchild craves for the love of a grandparent—and how mutual those feelings can be.

But what often happens is that many grandparents, because they are at a great distance or are hampered by the grandchild's parents, or because they do not want to interfere, or because they are just not interested, choose not to become involved with their grandchildren, only to remain locked into their own worlds. In May, 1990, ABC Nightly News reported that one-third of grandparents see their children only two or three times a year. A lot of them feel useless. Insensitivity to the needs and aspirations of their grandchildren easily results.

Too many grandparents fail to realize that grandchildren, and incidentally grandparents also, lose out by not being involved in one another's lives. The children are deprived primarily of emotional supports, for example, from someone who is special in their lives, though not of their immediate family, who is willing to go that extra step with them whenever no one else will, or someone who knows and treats them as "okay" in spite of their faults or mistakes, or not being able to reach the heights of other people's expectations. Grandchildren need someone other than their parents to count on, to trust, and to entrust their concerns to, no matter how big or small. They need those extra people who will celebrate their achievements and cheer them on to new challenges. They need an expanded sense of belonging that helps give them an appreciation of who they are. All of these factors help make a child fully alive. Grandparents have the potential to give freely and lovingly of these precious intangibles.

How can grandparents, if they do not react instinctively, achieve this breakthrough? If they show love, they will find love in their own hearts and in the hearts of others. By giving a little from their reserves of time and energy and by seizing the moments that opportunity presents, they enrich and energize their own lives in launching newcomers on the journey of life— ones who will carry on long after them.

Fostering New Visions

Would it not be wonderful if, besides one's own parents and siblings, there would also be special people in children's lives, to get happily excited whenever they say their first words, cheer them on as they take their first steps, show delight whenever they see them, or congratulate them when they do well in school or college. These manifestations convey an important message to the child—that they are special and worthwhile.

Children never run out of their need for encouragement. Someone, with the time and patience, who willingly lets them try new things certainly enhances the child's potential for growth and development. Confidence comes even if the first attempts end in failure. Not to be afraid to make mistakes enables one to learn from mistakes and to accept setbacks with a calm perspective and even with a sense of humor. Achievement progresses naturally. By the tone of their voice and the look on their face, nurturing people make a child feel the thrill of discovery and the openness to reasonable risk.

Expert nurturers are these big-hearted persons filled with love and a willingness to give someone a chance to become what they are meant to be in this life and the next. They accept and foster human uniqueness. Their breakthrough consists in the insight that the human heart—theirs in particular—has a true capacity for this congenial task. Children need all the help they can get in becoming fully alive persons. Grandparents, besides parents and siblings, are the persons closest to their grandchildren. As "grand" parents they have a major role to play, especially as nurturers. Being seasoned in nurturing, they can participate in guiding their grandchildren and awakening their capacities for wonder, learning, and loving. Nurturing ensures the fertile foundation for personal development.

Consider the quiet influence that the grandfather of actress and singer Debbie Reynolds had on her life and career.[4] Grandpa Harman, a lay Baptist minister and railroad man, was strong and handsome with broad shoulders and a prominent nose. He made life a joy for her. When he came from work, he would set her on his lap and tell her stories. The stories would be about the life and disciples of Jesus and sometimes just about his day on the railroad. To Debbie, he was a very loving man, and she felt that he treasured her. She remembers holding on to his large hands and fingers; his hugs that made her feel warm and sheltered.

On Sundays her grandfather would take her to church. The whole congregation would watch as they walked down the aisle together to put pennies in the basket. She, a tiny little girl, was so proud to be at his side. In fact, her grandfather probably gave her the confidence that helped to launch her career.

Even now Debbie can vividly picture the scene as her grandpa would place her up on the altar where she would sing a song he had taught her: "This little light of mine; I'm gonna let it shine." Debbie's first audience—her grandpa and grandma, her mother and half the church—would be in tears at the sight of such a darling child and she loved it! Who could deny the ongoing influence of this nurturing grandparent as she faced the difficulties and setbacks of a career in show business?

Knowing that a prescription for a healthy child presupposes a reservoir of love, grandparents who are part of the immediate circle of a child's family life are the ones who have what it takes to respond to this newcomer with a warm welcome. As the child journeys through life, they can provide an ongoing cushion of supportive care and attention. In such a way grandparents will be contributing to the building of a strong foundation so acutely needed in meeting the demands and challenges of modern day living.

A Closer Look

With the disintegration and fragmentation of family life, children need, more than ever before, emotional support in addition to that of their parents. Today's children are finding themselves helpless victims in situations brought about by their parents' problems, family conditions, or society's failures.

"It is not easy being a kid today" is what the Children's Defense Fund's 1988 Census data's annual report on the years 1985-1988 reveal. Consider, for example, what happens to children in America in each day:

2,795	Teenagers become pregnant. (1,106 of them later have abortions; 372 later miscarry.)
1,027	Babies are exposed *in utero* to drugs or alcohol.
67	Babies under 1 month old die.
105	Babies under 1 year old die.
211	Children are arrested for drug abuse.
437	Children are arrested for drinking and drunk driving.
10	Children die from gunshot wounds.
30	Children are wounded by gunfire.
135,000	Children bring a gun to school
1,512	Teenagers commit suicide.
3,288	Children run away from home.
1,629	Children are in adult jails.[5]

President George Bush insisted: "What those 'left out' need most is a relationship with someone who cares." Grandparents can be some of those thousand points of light—reaching out to younger persons before deterioration takes place. They can begin to do so at the birth of a child.

Trying to meet the everyday demands of living is no easy task. Parents find themselves confronted by very stressful situations. Often mothers are forced to seek employment outside the home in order to make ends meet. Some women, however, choose to pursue a professional career. As a consequence, many children are left to the care of persons who may not have a personal interest in them. Children in many day-care centers experience a quick turnover of caretakers. In some instances, children are being raised by children. As a result, the personal attention that a child needs at early stages in their development is lacking.

Grandparents can fill in the gaps of these day-to-day inadequacies. In one of the Regenerative Grandparenting workshops that I gave, an older grandmother told how she would drop by a day-care center periodically to spend time with her grandson.

"Sometimes I would bring something for all the children to share. Once I brought a frog. Now, whenever I come through the door, they all blurt out: 'Hello, Grandma.' "It makes me feel so good to know that I've become their Grandma, too."

This grandmother discovered how hungry children are for a caring "grand" person in their lives. By gaining this insight into her role as "nurturer," she subsequently made more of an effort to give her loving attention to other children as well.

Child development research reveals abundant information about the needs of children. We know, on one hand, that perceptual development of the child begins in the mother's womb and that after birth its further development is fostered by how the people in the child's life respond to the child—what spoken and unspoken messages the child perceives from others. Do they, for example, make a fuss over the child or demonstrate pleasure with its presence? Does the tone of their voice sound enthusiastic as they greet the child? All of these responses contribute to the sense of self that is in the process of being formed in the psyche of the child. They also influence the way judgments will be made later on.

As the child begins to accumulate a host of messages, some of which may be negative ones—such as, ignoring the child or treating it negligently—a sense of self and of others is formed. The child also attaches meaning to the sensations accompanying the experience which, in turn, contribute to the complexus of perceptions that lead to judgments. The ability to make sound judgments enables humans to grow to maturity.[6]

Ashley Montague reminds us that all reality is relational and that all relationships are enlarged and enriched in proportion to the sensitivity with which they are perceived and lived. To be sensitive is to be alive; and the more healthily sensitive one is to the world in which one lives the more alive one is. Grandparents help sensitize the child for wondering, learning, loving, and aspiring.

Given these findings, grandparents cannot afford to ignore or underestimate the importance of time, attention, care, and interaction that is directed toward a grandchild from the earliest stages of its life. A grandchild whose grandparent plays a role in this area is truly enriched. Imagine what a lasting influence a grandparent can have on a child, even in its infancy. All the positive messages a grandparent can send the baby—a loving cuddle which fosters security, the singing of songs, or just being there as a caring presence—blend together to provide a loving atmosphere for the developing child.

One baby boy in Pittsburgh, Pennsylvania, is experiencing this kind of nurturing from over one hundred unofficial aunts and grandmothers. They sit with him, sing to him, feed and nurture him. Afflicted with fetal alcohol syndrome and drug addicted, two-day old Brian (a foster child) was welcomed into the hearts and home of the Sisters of Divine Providence, a Catholic congregation of women religious. It is their hope that the love they give to Brian will give him a second chance in life.

Already love is at work. At two months of age, he tips the scale at nine pounds and is growing stronger and healthier. The sisters look forward to parenting and grandparenting other needy children. As highly qualified educators, they understand the consequences of a lack of nurturing early in life. Without personal nurturing, a child is unable to enter into intimate relationships as an adult.

Psychologist Brenda Hunter of northern Virginia knows from her own past the pain of this deprivation. Brenda traces her mother's inability to nurture to her "missing out" as one of eight children vying for the attention of an alcoholic father. Left with such an emotional legacy, Brenda's own marriage ended—leaving her alone with two babies. Thus began her inner journey that forced her to confront her past. In L'Abri, a Christian community in Ealing, London, she found the nurturing that she had never had and the possibility of unconditional love that led to her own healing. Some twenty years later at the age of 50, she obtained her Ph.D. from Georgetown University and was on her way to sharing her insights into the healing process with others who like herself had been deprived of nurturing in their early years. Her experience has prompted her to form in the United States a national organization, Home by Choice, which carries on similar work in counseling full-time mothers.

Brenda says of children: "For a child, absence generates profound feelings of rejection and a yearning for love that can dominate the whole of life."[7]

Just as electricity depends on voltage, so our lives depend upon the force of nurturing love. Jesus of Nazareth knew this well. As a lasting expression of his intense love for his flock, he gave himself in the eucharist as a reminder of his constant presence. He taught us that the strength of such love prevails even after death. Jesus never gives up on us. Like him, a loving grandparent never gives up on a grandchild.

I can relate well to the idea of love prevailing even after death. My grandfather is responsible for that. Grandpa was a fun-loving man. He had a way of communicating through his actions what was not always so clearly conveyed by his words. As a young man he had emigrated to this country and his

speech reflected a combination of the "mother tongue" blend-
ed into the English language.

Fortunately, Grandpa lived within walking distance of us.
This was to my advantage for I could pay him a visit whenever I
felt like it. To me he was like honey in a jar. I could tell he loved
me whenever he sat me upon his lap and gave me his total
attention. I was never on the sidelines with him. Then he would
begin playing a game with me. Of course, his words were in a
language that was foreign to me. Somehow that did not seem to
matter in the least.

What did make a difference was that Grandpa knew what
kids were all about and acted on it. He created a rapport that
made me feel that of all the grandchildren, he liked me the
best. Only after his death years later, did I discover that my sister had exactly the same feeling of being "number one" with
him that I myself had.

Grandpa was truly a "one-on-one" grandfather. That
makes me wonder how much of an influence he was in
enabling me to have a kindly spirit toward life, and toward children in particular.

All children need a constancy of love in their lives. That
can come in the form of encouragement. Recently, the need for
building self-esteem (one's opinion as to one's own worth) has
been given special notice. State commissions from Maryland
and Virginia were looking for psychological reasons for school
dropouts, teenage pregnancy, drug abuse, and violent crime.
They found that the lack of a good self-image to be the most
common characteristic of these troubled youngsters.

According to one theory, without a good self-image people
are less able to deal with life's obstacles and challenges and are
more likely to turn disappointment over failures into self-
destructive behavior. Members of the state commissions felt
that the task of addressing this concern has fallen to them
because the family and society at large are failing to pass on values to the next generation to help them lead happy, successful
lives.

The State of Virginia's task force came out with two hundred recommendations for raising self-esteem. These included suggestions such as: take time to praise others when they do a good job; don't be too critical; and share good news with others to enhance their ability to achieve.[8]

Self-esteem is strengthened by nurturing, but it must rest on a strong commitment to values. Without moral principles, self-esteem is empty and short-lived. In light of this truth a former District of Columbia Superior Court judge and associate director of the Office of National Drug Control Policy, Reggie B. Walton, lamented the fact that the importance of values and morals for many has been reduced to "what is best for me regardless of what effect one's conduct has on the rest of society." He believes this deterioration of values and morals to be the real root cause of the drug crisis that is now plaguing the country. The message that we need to send our youth about the value of doing what is right is this: working hard, even though success comes slowly, is the only sure way.[9] Without a principled life there is no true self-esteem.

Educating for values was further emphasized by the National Commission on Children, a thirty-six member group established by Congress in 1987 and charged with assessing "the status of children nationwide and with developing a policy agenda to improve their health and well-being." During the meeting, they discussed the role of public institutions in teaching values.

Virtually everyone on the commission agreed that the family is the best place for moral education, and that steps need to be taken to strengthen family life.[10]

Grandparents who possess a trained eye, are able to see where the cracks are in a family household. Sometimes children fall through those cracks and need a helping hand—someone to reach out to them, to help them to get back on the right path, or even just to let them know that someone out there cares.

At a time when families are described as living under separate roofs—going to two employers for money, to different schools for education, to fast food restaurants for dinner—we wonder who's raising our children. Who's in charge? Ralph

Nader claims that corporations have become more important in raising children than parents. (McDonald's is feeding them; HBO and Disneyland are entertaining them.) Mealtime has been reduced to individual servings, and weekends are reserved for errands.

Grandparents should not wait for problems to occur for them to step in and lend a hand. An involved grandparent anticipates the needs of a child and does something about them. Their natural love for their grandchildren can be a catalyst for many good things to follow.

For example, grandparents, particularly those who live nearby, can use their voices for encouragement or in recognition of some accomplishment. They may even offer a friendly smile. A perceptive grandparent quickly notes when a child is "down" or worried and responds in a caring, supportive way. Sometimes what grandparents do will be indirect (lending financial assistance for a family to get back on its feet), and at other times they will take the initiative to make a more obvious difference (substituting for a sick parent) in the lives of children. Grandparents are always needed.

Surrogate Parenting

"I have a Mommy and her name is Grammy," sang five year old Kayla.

A growing number of grandparents are putting their lives on "hold" to become parents for the second time around. As far back as the seventeenth century the grandmother of Sir Isaac Newton, famed for his discovery of the law of gravity, assumed responsibility for bringing up her grandson.

All across the nation many grandparents, including great-grandparents, are rearing grandchildren either on a part-time or a full-time basis. In fact, of the nation's 63.8 million children, 3.2 million live with their grandparents and tens of thousands have no parent present at all. Furthermore, fifty percent of the children in the Head Start Program in Delaware County, Media, Pennsylvania, are being raised by grandparents. Moreover without legal guardianship or custody, these grandparents cannot get medical attention, health insurance, or school admission for the children. There is difficulty, too, with Medicaid, Aid to Families with Dependent Children, and foster-care payments.[11]

Many grandparents, their active parenting days presumably over, are now being called upon to make the same kind of sacrifice all over again—this time as surrogate parents. Now they are assuming the role of primary caregivers for their grandchildren. In order to prevent their grandchildren from having to go into foster homes to be raised by total strangers in what could become constantly changing households, many grandparents have opted to step in and take charge at great cost to themselves physically, emotionally, economically, and temporally. "I'd rather have them," says Johnnie Mae Short, "than worry about them." Despite her heart attack several years ago, Johnnie Mae and her husband are raising three grandchildren.

Unlike foster parents, grandparents raising their natural grandchildren receive minimal federal or state support. Some, however, do qualify for Aid to Families with Dependent Children. But the multifaceted burden of providing extended support and personal care rests solely on them.

These very special grandparents face obstacles that test their call to unconditional love. Sometimes a feeling of personal guilt might overtake them: "Where did I go wrong in raising my own kids?" or "What did I do to cause this?"

"Parenting" grandparents seem to agree that they do not have the energy they once had. Few would disagree that the most stressful task that faces them today is rearing children. Yet many, especially widowed grandmothers, willingly assume this responsibility. And the results can be impressive, no matter what level of education they have attained. Their grandchildren remain eternally grateful. Such was the effect on John Ray of Washington, D.C.

John Ray was raised by his African-American grandparents. When John was twelve, his mother, a single parent, moved to Florida in search of work, and left him in the care of his grandparents who lived in poor Echols County, Georgia.

Grandfather Ray was the only father John had ever known. For John, his grandfather, though not quite six feet tall, was a giant of a man. He wore overalls and work shoes, chewed tobacco, and could spit farther and swear better than any man in Echols County. He was John's hero. Unfortunately, he could not read or write, but according to John, he knew how to train a boy to be a man of honesty, determination, and courage. Nor could his grandmother read the Bible—or read at all—but she knew its teachings and passed them on to John. Her faith in God was her foundation.

Both grandparents handed on these old-fashioned values. Today as a councilman in the nation's capital, John Ray looks back with the realization that although he grew up in poverty, his grandparents had instilled in him something far greater than money could buy, sound values and a strong desire for improving the society in which he lives.[12]

Often surrogate grandparents find that the relationship with their friends gets disrupted. Long-time friends with more free time still expect the spontaneous meetings and phone calls without giving a thought to the new scheduling demands. Caring for a child might mean declining a quick invitation to join friends in the evening, because there is no time or money to get a babysitter. Such impasses happening once too often tend to leave the grandparent with fewer calls and fewer friends and a sense of losing out on the hard-earned peace and joy of retirement. Friends need to understand.

Coping with a child's problems in school can prove challenging. Children may have difficulty learning because of poor concentration. Children worry about their parents to whom they still feel a strong attachment, regardless of how badly they were treated. They still hope their parents will change and return to take care of them. Children are often torn in two ways. On the one hand, children become quite dependent upon grandparents. They worry about them for fear they might be abandoned again. On the other hand, they can feel embarrassed at the age of their grandparents when they see other kids and their parents. Sometimes their peers may even tease them about this difference.

Grandparents who parent will be doing a favor for themselves as well as for their grandchildren by taking time out for themselves. This is a must. Going to the hairdresser's, visiting friends, taking a weekly painting class, playing bingo occasionally, or joining a bowling team all help. One of the grandmothers in a support group underscored this need by saying, "When you're good to yourself, you can be good to others."

Very important to the success of surrogate grandparenting are the support groups that are being formed around the country. Sharing with other grandparents in similar circumstances lightens the individual burden. People are able to confront the common feelings of inadequacy and guilt and to exchange with others their difficulties and coping strategies. Strengthened by their mutual understanding, they are better able to carry out the demanding task of child care with new realizations and renewed spirit.

Some groups begin simply when a concerned grandparent places an advertisement in the newspaper evoking responses from other similarly situated grandparents. Other groups are being formed by family counselors and social workers or the clergy. Here is a sampling of groups, some with chapters, already formed around the country: From Generation To Generation, in Milwaukee, Wisconsin; Grandparents As Parents (GAP), in East Palo Alto, California; Grandparents Against Immorality and Neglect, in Shreveport, Louisiana; Grandparents Raising Grandchildren, in Colleyville, Texas; and Second Time Around Parents, in Media, Pennsylvania. The members attest to the fact that group support has changed their lives.

What do this special breed of nurturing grandparents derive from it all? It is more than just filling a need by taking on a satisfying but burdensome duty. Paula Browne best describes it by saying: "These kids give you so much love—more than your own kids—because you've taken them out of the depths they've been in."[13]

Part-time Solutions

Grandparents willing to help a single parent can find themselves taking over more and more responsibilities. This new allocation often means that grandparents are primary caregivers for most of the time. With such an overlap, grandparents need a clearly articulated "job description" in order to avoid pitfalls that would be harmful not only to the child but also to the adults.

When Ruth's daughter became widowed, she found herself acting as a full-time parent while her daughter worked during the day. The problem was that three year old Billy was too active a match for his grandmother who, although only fifty-eight, had severe arthritis, which sharply limited her activity. The constant demands made upon her frail health left her resentful at having to be a parent again. Mother and daughter were beginning to squabble and Billy, usually good-natured, became disruptive.

On a visit to her doctor, Ruth expressed the hope that her condition would improve so that she could handle these new pressures. The doctor made a simple suggestion: get a babysitter for the morning hours when Billy was most active. Ruth was able to get an older woman in to help. Although Ruth stayed in the house, she was relatively free in the mornings and could manage in the afternoon until her daughter returned. Months of tension could have been avoided if, as soon as problems surfaced, mother and daughter had talked things over. As it was, both contributed to the babysitter and both felt secure about Billy since the grandmother was at home most of the time.

The solution to problems like this one requires that the grandmother does not swallow her feelings or conceal her difficulties, but gently dialogues with her daughter about what can best accommodate the interest of all three. Mutual understanding and the coming up with some good ideas is the usual result.

A different aspect of the problem and, from the perspective of the child, a more fundamental one is the question of control. Even in a two-parent family, the lines of authority may be out of harmony. But when someone comes in from outside, even someone as familiar as a grandparent, there is often not only confusion on the part of the child but also an attempt to play one adult against the other. The result may be competition between parent and grandparent. Here clear lines of authority are necessary from the beginning. Normally, the parent has the last word. Sometimes, however, the grandparent may be the only one in charge for long periods. Then, when the parent returns, conflicts may arise from all three, grandparent, parent, and child. A mature dialogue with nurturing as its goal helps resolve these tensions.

Grandparents who, in advance, take steps to avoid potential problems in parenting find the experience most rewarding. Grandchildren have a real need for the love and attention that grandparents can give. Grandparents who feel needed can find new meaning in their lives: the opportunity to be a sound influence in the lives of their grandchildren.

As a social service worker, I found myself paying periodic visits to a household in which the grandmother was a full-time parent to her daughter's two children, a four- and five-year old, during the day. Besides this task, she also cared for her invalid husband who was confined to bed. Yet the house was filled with love. The children were happy, playful, and cooperative. Disagreements were settled with ease. As I studied the situation carefully, I discovered that this grandmother fostered in her grandchildren a loving sensitivity and respect by how she spoke to them, how she guided them in relating to their bedridden grandfather, and how she paid special interest to each one. These two grandchildren were learning a lesson of care and service from experiencing a grandmother who loved them and expected them to share her love for another. I noticed this especially in the kindly way they related to their sick grandfather who, unable to speak, beamed whenever they came into the room. All my visits to this household revealed the formative influence a nurturing grandparent can have on her family.

After all, whether as a full-time surrogate or a part-time helper, a grandparent should be above all a nurturer. Problems inevitably arise. But love, not domination, is the means by which the help given channels a young life toward fulfillment.

Major Crises

Grandparents today are in the news more than ever before. For many families, they have become a necessity. Separation and divorce, illness and death have shown that grandparents are the second line of security for grandchildren.

Statistics today reveal a trend running counter to the multi-generational family unit. The growing emergence of single-parent families affects half of all children born since the late 1970s. Whatever the cause—widowed or divorced parents, parents incapable of child care due to financial or job problems, illness or institutionalization—the single parent usually turns to a grandparent for help. Most often it is the grandmother.

With the high rate of divorce a serious threat to the American family, grandparents are often the only guarantee of emotional stability for the children. Grandparents can make it possible both financially and psychologically for a single parent to preserve a family context for the children. A single mother or a single father might not be able to manage at all without the help of their parents. Without these grandparents, the grandchildren would lose the sense of love and security so vital for healthy and mature adjustment.

Divorce usually puts grandparents and grandchildren in an awkward situation. There is an understandable tendency for each set of grandparents to side with their own son or daughter. The best interests of the child, however, call for all grandparents to remain as neutral and as amicable as possible. Although it may be difficult for grandparents to maintain the same relationship with their grandchildren, they should try to continue the pre-breakup pattern as much as possible until a new one emerges.

If grandparents find that the particular pattern for visits with the grandchild has been changed, they should adjust to this different schedule. Often patience will pay off in a better relationship. Grandchildren, whatever the merits of the parent's case, should never be used as weapons or prizes. Children are not pawns. Each is a unique person, whose destiny must be fully respected.

Divorce is not the only tragedy affecting the family. The increasing incidence of the abuse and neglect of children in today's family has forced many grandmothers to take over. Some cases are the result of the current harsh economic realities but others, the more shocking ones, are the fruit of the drug culture that is devastating many American families.

These prevailing conditions have even affected the role of today's black grandmother. Forty years ago and earlier, the black grandmother was the pillar of support for the extended family, especially in rural areas of the south. Grandmothers were usually the ones who instilled values and kept the family together. In fact, when the grandmother was young, often the great-grandmother remained the stabilizing force in the family.

With the movement to cities and urbanization many black grandmothers experienced a change in their role. This became even more true with the spiraling increase in teenage pregnancy. The problem has worsened in view of the fact that grandmothers, among the urban poor, often are under thirty-five years of age and lack a firm, sound formation from their own mothers. What is worse is that many of the very young grandmothers are themselves drug addicted.

The net result of these destabilizing conditions is that many grandmothers and great-grandmothers have given up and are not playing their expected role of instilling values and holding families together. Many have not learned the skills needed to help those who are dependent on them. This situation has important implications for black children.[14]

Unfortunately, while the need for nurturing remains critical for black children, the role of the black grandmother is declining. As values change in society, many blacks turn from their strong family traditions. Grandmothers no longer live in the same house or in the same community. The question is who can black children count on when all else fails? Often, they cannot even find their grandparents.

The most disturbing aspect of this crisis is the plight of the children who are born of mothers addicted to crack-cocaine. Washington, D.C. police sergeant Peter Banks of the youth division, noted that during his experience of twenty years on the force, this is the first time that he sees kids being born without families and being left without mothers. According to him, nobody is holding them, nobody is giving them any love, nobody is teaching them any moral values.

Many black grandmothers have courageously risen to the occasion. But the demand for such persons exceeds the supply. One such grandmother, Mrs. Gordon, felt the responsibility to take up where the parents left off. Her five grandchildren depend upon her for survival since their own parents are too immature to care for them. This grandmother was told that all her grandchildren were high-risk babies—who have or who are likely to develop medical problems or learning disabilities as a result of their mother's drug use. She struggles to give her grandchildren another chance at life.

Caring for her grandchildren involved quitting her part-time job because she could not afford a babysitter. Mrs. Patricia Gordon even used up her savings on the children until she could receive financial assistance. Grandmother Gordon has no idea how long she will be taking care of her grandchildren, but says she has considered the possibility that she may be involved until they are grown. "I feel God is not going to fail my grandchildren," she said.[15] Nor is Mrs. Gordon.

Deep love and a strong will accomplishes wonders. When the life or well-being of a grandchild is at stake, a grandparent can rise to the occasion. A Moscow grandmother is a striking example of undaunted love working against almost insurmountable odds for her year-old grandson, Kirill.

Given reports about the inoperable tumor on his brain and the decision of the Soviet doctors not to operate, Zoya Zdanovskaya could not abandon hope for her only grandson and the son of her only son. Believing that someone in the United States would be able to help, Zoya, alone in her cramped apartment, wrote a letter on December 7, 1988, to the Voice of America. That letter was the catalyst that brought together the Soviet child, a team of highly skilled medical professionals in the Bronx, a foundation executive in Texas, and a Soviet-American grandmother from Brooklyn who acted as translator for Kirill's mother and grandmother and helped support them.

Fourteen weeks and two days later, a benign tumor the size of an orange was removed from the child's terribly swollen head one day after he turned two. News of Kirill's operation reached the president of the International Craniofacial Foundations in Dallas. The president of the foundations began a process that led to further help for Kirill. Eventually, a medical exchange program between the Soviets and Americans developed that would treat children.

Zoya claims this could never have taken place before Gorbachev and Glasnost. Dr. Goodrich, and the Soviet-American grandmother see it somewhat differently. Both agree that this child would never have shown up here without a person of Zoya's force and direction. The political conditions were right, but as the doctor insisted: "She was the moving force."[16]

Love Makes a Difference

The nurturing instinct and the natural love of a grandparent rose to the occasion in Grandma Gordon's life and in Mrs. Zdnovskaya's. Many other children are not so fortunate as to have a caring and determined grandparent take responsibility when parents fail to meet their primary one. Child-care workers agree that neglect damages a child's self-esteem and personality. Neglected children have internal scars that may last the rest of their lives.

A grandparent's love can be transformative to a child, as the family of Tara Handy saw happening before their eyes, only to see everything end in tragedy. Tara was a beautiful and happy four-year-old child who was severely disabled. Although she was not even able to scratch herself, she showed a wide range of emotions. Tara's family attributed her wholehearted capacity for loving to the love she received not only from her parents and her brother, but especially from her grandmother.

"Tara would cry out in joy at her grandmother's voice." These were the words spoken by one of her parents before the judge sentenced the sixty-eight year old grandmother who had pleaded guilty to involuntary manslaughter. While admittedly drunk, she had accidently killed the disabled girl with an overdose of adult sleeping pills.

The distraught grandmother, torn by grief, could hardly get her own words out. As she spoke betweens sobs that made her shoulders heave, she tried to make sense out of her granddaughter's death. "Horrible, reckless, terrible, I loved her as much as anyone I've ever loved in my life."

Tara's own father, an economist, in letters to the judge, reaffirmed the loving relationship between Tara, who suffered from cerebral palsy, and her grandmother: "There wasn't a shadow of doubt in my mind that Tara's death was an accident," wrote her father. "Tara's love for her grandmother was clear for all to see; so, too, was her grandmother's love for her evident in all the things she did with Tara and for her."

The grandmother's legs gave out as she slipped into a chair. A moment of silence followed. The judge was moved by the grief of this grandmother and the series of recent tragedies that had befallen the family. Looking at the grandmother, he gave his sentence, one that her attorney called stunning: he put her on probation for eighteen months and ordered her to do 250 hours of community service and continue treatment for alcoholism.[17]

This traumatic crisis had a satisfying ending. But it points out the risks involved in all parenting. Accidents occur and so do abuses. Bad things happen to the good and the bad and the negligent. Would that we could escape safely from every crisis. But there is risk in all loving, in all living. If risks are unavoidable, let them be faced in a good cause. In the long run, good will prevail.

Nurturing in the Four Seasons

Nurturing is the all-pervading quality of a grandparent-grandchild relationship. Sometimes it is done intentionally. At other times it is the caring dimension that accompanies all that takes place between a loving grandparent and a grandchild.

Nature provides opportunities for a grandparent and grandchild to foster the caring attitude and loving response. Though the rhythms of life and the rotation of the seasons of the year bring with it many changes, the cycles remain constant. It is the nature of a cycle to repeat its themes, but in new ways. From birth to death, we find ourselves conditioned by the changing seasons. Yet, year after year we are never quite the same as we change with the seasons.

The changes we undergo are related to the stages of our development—a big snowstorm does not mean quite the same thing to the father or mother driving to work as it does to the child getting a school holiday. Cooperating with the seasons calls for new experiences and new insights as we reach into ourselves to become the best that we can. Because we are a people of purpose and destiny, we need to extend this care to things outside ourselves; that mission includes caring for all creation—everything that inhabits our planet.

These two interlocking themes, helping human beings and saving the planet, can be taught by grandparents as they nurture their grandchildren. To realize that we are connected with all of nature and creation in this pattern of movement and change is to arrive at an important insight. Grandparents who are aware of this truth can be the gentle guides attuned both to youngster's development and the seasons of the year. Grandparents can instill an appreciation of nature and a sense of responsibility in young people for what will be their earthly environment for the future.

Where do grandparents begin? One way is by looking at the rich possibilities that each season holds for relating in a deeply caring way—with warmth and closeness—to the younger generation. A good start is to consider each season as a backdrop on a changing stage where love plays out its productive dialogue.

SUMMER

Summertime affords a great beginning. School is out. Grandchildren and grandparents are fairly free. Time together is a time for revitalizing a relationship—strengthening cherished bonds or building new ones—particularly when there are stepgrandchildren. The parents ordinarily are still at work. This is an ideal time for grandparents to offer children a chance for an extended visit either at their home or away.

Interested grandparents don't miss other opportunities for spending valued time with the younger generation. One family on the East coast began the annual tradition of inviting grandparents who lived at a distance to join them on a week's vacation at a state park. Beginning with the birth of the first child and continuing with the next one, they all shared a family vacation. Outdoors in the beautiful mountains of West Virginia, the grandparents and grandchildren experienced the beauty of nature and made discoveries about other aspects of their rustic setting. What a sacrifice it was at first for grandma and her curious ten year old granddaughter to get up at six o'clock in the morning to go bird watching with the state ranger. Sharing an enthusiasm for learning about the wide variety of birds, each with its own song, fashioned a special bond between the two of them. An added treat was the fun that came from the challenge of not making a sound that would frighten away the birds before all could get a closer look. Their having a special experience provided them with food for conversation and shared memories, an intimacy to which others were not privy.

Meanwhile the grandfather, who was suffering from arthritis which impaired his walking, made every effort to take the hike through the woods and even go horseback riding with his grandchildren. Spurred on by a desire to be actively involved with them, he soon discovered the rewards of togetherness in a revitalized spirit, which lasted even on his return home. Incidentally, his arthritic knees improved too.

Repeating a family vacation each year or doing some other nurturing experiences further reinforces this intergenerational bonding. Years later unforeseen circumstances regarding the precarious health conditions of these grandparents intervened. Their situation threatened their traveling that year. As soon as the children—now teenagers—learned of this, they immediately telephoned and pleaded for them to reconsider. Their actions manifest the treasured relationship which was brought about by the two grandparents who had seized summertime opportunities to give extra love and attention to their grandchildren and ended up by fostering their own interests as well.

Today there are places available specifically for grandparents and grandchildren to go camping together. Organizations such as the Foundation for Grandparenting in Cohasset, Massachusetts, and Elderhostel in Canada provide such opportunities. The experiences of grandparents and grandchildren during those times prove to be truly beneficial for each. The special closeness between grandparents and grandchildren takes on deep and lasting meaning.

Autumn

With the arrival of autumn grandparents and grandchildren find themselves in the season of harvest time—pumpkins, candy apples, turkeys, ghosts and goblins, and football games. Using themes of the season enables grandparents to plan fun-filled adventures that will long be remembered.

This is the time of the year for grandparents to encourage creativity in their grandchildren; for example, by inviting them to share in decorating the house for Halloween. Letting the grandchild take the lead in deciding the expression on the face to be carved on the jack-o-lantern can affirm the child's role in producing a centerpiece for all to admire. A mature child can even participate in the carving. Writing the child's name on the pumpkin enhances the feeling of accomplishment and the value of joint projects.

In doing things together, opportunities abound for the grandparent to help the youngster feel lovable and capable. By positive words, gestures, and a warm presence that express an encouraging and comfortable atmosphere grandparents nourish the growth potential of a child. Gramps Ken, a wiry retiree and hiker from Harrisburg, Pennsylvania has his own way of helping. He especially likes autumn. He and his grandson, Patrick, always make it a point to go leaf hunting together, collecting the most colorful and varied ones, identifying and labeling them. Not a year goes by without their marveling at the beauty of creation and learning more about the varying face of nature.

WINTER

Wintery days can provide magic moments for grandchildren to remember. Carol, now fifty, remembers walking to visit her grandparents many years ago. She can still picture the snow that covered the trees and that was piled along the street as she shuffled her small feet through the drifts. Her mother had bundled her into a snowsuit, with a scarf draped around her neck. But by the time she reached her grandparent's house her hands seemed half-frozen. Only grandad was home when she arrived. She could see it as if it were yesterday, his tall, thin frame as he opened the door and peered down at her.

"He showed a tender concern for the little girl who had trudged through the snow on a cold day just to visit him and Granny," she remembered. "I could tell he was just sitting down to have a hot cup of coffee when I surprised him. While my coat was still on, he took off my mittens and began to blow on my cold little hands and rub them to make them warm."

"Then Grandad went over to the stove to make me a cup of hot cocoa which he then placed on the table near where I stood. As he turned around to get a cup for himself, I happened to knock my cocoa over. It began trickling onto the floor much to my chagrin. Startled by this, I quickly picked up the cup, moved in the direction of the door, and announced that now I had to leave. Because Grandad's hearing was impaired and because I was away from the table, I had hoped that he was not aware of what had just happened. 'But you just came,' he said, appearing surprised, while holding his cup of coffee. 'I think my mother wants me,' I said sheepishly. Somehow I noticed the twinkle in his eye and the chuckle in his voice as he said 'Okay, okay.' At that, I rapidly left."

Forty-four years later Carol still savors the warm feeling and gentle consideration that came from her undemanding grandfather. She realizes now that her grandfather must have noticed. "I treasure all the more the memory of his tender concern for that chilled and embarrassed little girl on that wintery day. Grandpa really loved me. I knew I counted with him."

As cold as winter can be, so can be the warmth generated by ordinary occasions made special because of what happens when a caring grandparent shares time with a grandchild. A few significant moments can color a person's whole life.

Opportunities for communicating love are always present. A nurturing spirit will recognize the right occasion. Being available makes the difference. Taking walks together while enjoying the sights of snow-covered objects and then sharing a cup of hot chocolate can enliven the spirits of a grandchild and grandparent. Winter sports, such as ice hockey, skiing, and ice-skating, afford an added treat—for spectators, too. On a less strenuous level, building a snowman dressed in an old hat and scarf or even taking a sled ride, can add delight to both lives. No matter, it is what happens when two people, one older, the other younger, come together that warms the heart with abiding love even in the dead of winter.

SPRING

For intergenerational bonding, spring is the most exciting time. Grandparents can use that time of year to stimulate the natural wonder common in children by enabling them to connect with the mysteries of nature and of life itself. By planting seeds and watching them grow, children and grandparents are able to identify with the cycles of life, involving death and rebirth. Dying, as a seed must do when placed in the ground, and then, after a period of time, emerging with new life—this is an ever-occurring motif throughout all creation, an archetypal idea that resonates in the hearts of young and old.

Fernando, short, fat, and energetic, had a wide array of flowers and vegetables growing in his backyard. The evident pleasure that he took in his neatly cared-for garden awakened in his six-year-old grandson, Marco, a yen for gardening. Watching the plants grow and the vegetables picked and eaten, the young boy begged his parents to let him have his own small plot of land.

With some help from his grandfather, Marco began his garden only to discover the ongoing need to care for and nurture what he had planted. Frequent watering, pulling up of weeds, and constructing a scarecrow to scare away the birds enabled Marco to experience many lessons transferrable to life. "To teach patience," Fernando observed, "teach gardening." Indeed, Marco soon found that for something to grow it takes time and that if he begins something, he must be responsible for it. Responsibility means time and energy and even sacrifice. If not, you get weeds, bugs, dried up roots, and rotten vegetables. By the end of the summer, Marco was glad his garden was small, but he felt like a little man when he could harvest its fruits.

Eleven years have passed away and so has Fernando. Seventeen year old Marco continues his spring planting and always includes his grandfather's favorites, zenias and red peppers. "Someday I'd like to teach gardening to my own grandchildren," he remarked pensively. Then he laughed, "At least to my children—when I finish college and when I get married. In the meantime, I'll just have to pull these weeds myself."

Keeping Youthful

Indeed, spring, the season of rebirth is the right season for us to end our discussion about opportunities for nurturing throughout the year. As the life cycle begins anew and as grand-parents observe the seeds of love maturing generation after generation, they appreciate their own role in the cultivation of the spirit.

Edith Cobb in describing the miracle of a child's develop-ment from its natural beginnings to its cultural fulfillment, noted that more than the power to think is needed. The child must learn to absorb love and to share love. A full life requires meanings and feelings. Otherwise the child remains egocentric, encapsulated in a lonely realm, never socially and spiritually alive.[18]

Grownups, too, need the experience of giving and receiv-ing love. The instinct for nurturing should never dry up, no matter how old one is. "In our innermost soul," Freud observed, "we are children and remain so for the rest of our lives." The child in us needs to love and be loved. Adults can preserve that dual love by giving themselves to others. In doing so, the rewards far exceed the trouble.

A grandparent's expression of nurturance is one of the best ways of releasing bottled-up energy. This unchanelled power is often revealed in the ungiving grandparent as a sense of meaninglessness or as a sunken or guilty feeling. But in beginning to give special attention and care to a young person, a grandparent soon discovers a new and transforming spirit. This caregiving can make a positive difference in one's physical and mental state. Many involved grandparents experience a renewed feeling of health and happiness.

Art Blakey, genius of jazz who died in 1990, exemplified this regenerative quality of nurturing. His spirit soared with the beat of his music. Speaking metaphorically, he once said, "If your heart don't beat, you're dead."[19]

His life reflected his words. He never retired from music or from life. In his wisdom he knew the value of relating to the younger generation. They needed him, but he needed them too: "I'm gonna stay with youngsters. When these get too old, I'm gonna get some younger ones. Keeps the mind active."

He often said that young musicians rejuvenated him, kept

him curious. (Thomas Jefferson experienced the same feedback from the young.) What the young people got in return from Art was not formal training but constant nurturing and the artistic room to stretch out and find themselves. With his nurturing approach, he focused on the untried musicians, or at least the unproven ones. In the process, Blakey groomed them for future leadership by encouraging them to write and find their own artistic voice. He forced his musicians to dig deep into themselves and play to their capacity. Many of them did. They carry his message: "Be true to yourselves," as his legacy to future generations of jazz musicians. Art Blakey lives on.

To conclude, grandchildren and grandparents need each other. In relating to one another, both call forth special gifts. Caring and involved grandparents can add an extra boost to a child who is just beginning its life's journey, for children need all the help they can get in growing into fully alive persons. In turn, grandparents satisfy their innate need to give of themselves and discover new meaning in their lives.

Where should grandparents begin? With a vision—a vision of how best to express their love. Affection, support, respect, fostering the child's physical, emotional, intellectual, and spiritual development are facets of this nurturing. At times grandparents might have to take the lead in helping out during a family crisis. This might mean helping out financially, lending emotional support, or even assuming parental responsibilities. It is never too late for grandparents to begin. Somewhere there is a child waiting for an older person to reach out and care for. Only by receiving love can a person learn to love, for the nature of love is to be passed on. The contribution of caring grandparents toward the young begins in the present and extends into the future. Ask anyone who has had the experience of such grandparents. They will tell you it is so. They know.

Nurturing is love in action. Love is mutually beneficial: lover and beloved both prosper. Without a nurturing heart, grandparents can make only a cold connection. They may give many gifts and much assistance, but without wholehearted loving, they miss out on what grandparenting is all about.

Nonetheless, nurturing alone does not suffice. Other qualities and actions are needed to help carry out this primary and loving function. Grandparents can give only what they have. But they can give so much more if, in addition to being nurturers, they act as historians, mentors, models of aging, and sages. It does not mean that grandparents are expected to be experts in these various areas, but that they should use the many strengths that they all have, so that their love for their grandchildren reaches a lasting fruition.

Tips on Communicating Love

1. Accept your grandchild for who she or he is. Respect each grandchild as a very special person. Try to discover something unique about each one and provide an opportunity to encourage its development. Believe in them. *Never* ridicule them. Compliment them often.

2. Take time to be with your grandchild. Plan a day together and include a new experience (trolley ride, fishing, a jazz concert, camping) and ones that support religious and family values (sing-alongs, a Fourth of July celebration, nameday and holy day celebrations, a first-time driver's license). Go for a walk and admire the plants and animals. Laugh together, sing together, play together, think together. Share a common secret. Adapt your behavior to the child's age and level of development.

3. Allow your grandchild to help you. Prepare a meal or dessert together. Go grocery shopping together and have them choose some foods.

4. Be patient, fair, and forgiving. Walk that "extra" mile with them. Keep your word to them. Show interest in what they have to say by making appropriate comments and asking questions. Listen attentively when they speak—making eye contact with them.

5. Show affection to each one. Warmly welcome them with enthusiasm and when departing. Tell them you love them

again and again. Hug, cuddle, and give them a warm pat. Take the initiative even if they don't.

6. When living at a distance keep in touch. Write, telephone, or send letters, cards, audio/video tapes about yourself or a picture album of yourself and your activities with a written or recorded explanation of each. Start a family newsletter and include information about all its members. Alternate special features on each grandchild.

2

GRANDPARENTS AS *FAMILY HISTORIANS:* RETRIEVING THE PAST

After describing the revolutionary upheavals occurring in Eastern Europe, President George Bush brought to a close his 1990 State of the Union Address with this appeal:

> Let me start with my generation—the grandparents out there. You are our living link to the past. Tell your grandchildren the story of struggles waged, at home and abroad. Of sacrifices freely made for freedom's sake. And tell your own story as well because every American has a story to tell.[1]

The president challenged all grandparents to be family historians. One might well ask, then, why is it necessary that grandparents should be historians? And how can they do so successfully? First of all, it is important to keep in mind that family history is primarily an account of nurturing through time—the successes and failures of love. And history must face squarely the truth of the past. What has happened is over, but to do something about it is always within our power. We retrieve the past, and if need be, redeem the past, so that we can perfect the future. Grandparents, with their feet in both worlds, can transform human existence.

Links to the Past

President Bush's phrase, "our living link with the past," gives the key. A recent event illustrates this point vividly. In January, 1990, for the first time an African American, Douglas Wilder, became the Governor of Virginia. Wilder, himself the grandson of slaves, was now the governor of a former slave state. At his inauguration, a black woman waited patiently in the massive crowd to catch a glimpse of the governor. She said that she just had to be there—for herself, for her children, and for her grandchildren. Here was a five generation link to the past: the woman's grandchildren linked to the governor's grandfather.

Grandparents can re-create the past by describing the things and events and people that they experienced in joy and sorrow. They can bring a forgotten world out of the darkness as it comes alive in the minds of later generations.

We learn of such grandparental influence from the biographies of persons who have made their mark in history. For example, the noted reporter, Edward R. Murrow, related that his maternal grandfather, Captain Van, was a great storyteller. Sitting in a rocker under a walnut tree, he would repeat, with very little prompting from his grandchildren, the old tales of life in the wilderness—people facing starvation and having to trap animals to stay alive.

Murrow's favorite story was one of Stonewall Jackson's being accidentally and fatally wounded by one of his own men just after the battle of Chancellorsville. Captain Van caught the stricken Jackson as he slipped from his horse and held the dying man in his arms. These stirring accounts filled the young boy with the love of American history and the skills of a true raconteur.[2]

What makes the past come alive is the sense of immediacy that only an eyewitness can give. Grandparents were there, and they can electrify their descendants by their true stories about things that influenced their lives and that happened before their listeners were born.

We listen to these stories because they explain us to ourselves. A need prompts us to satisfy our curiosity over how we have become what we are now. Cicero wrote: "Not to know what happened before one was born is always to be a child." And George Santayana seems to have paraphrased Cicero: "Where experience is not retained. . . infancy is perpetual."³

To understand ourselves, we must delve into our twofold history. We have a personal, familial history, and we have a social, cultural history. To understand ourselves as individuals, we must also understand ourselves as members of a community, actually of many communities, cultural, political and religious. We may start with the personal but the questions we ask lead us to the larger sociocultural context. Ideally, in both there is a strong religious dynamism.

Grandparents are the windows of time. They know how things used to be and can trace the changes that have occurred over the years. Seeing the past through their eyes we begin to understand our present and fashion our future. As the poet T.S. Eliot wrote: "Time present and time past/ Are both perhaps present in time future/ And time future contained in time past."⁴ Grandparents can link past, present, and future—if they are willing to try. Let us look at some of these unpretentious historians.

Anthony, a tall eighty-one year old man known as "Poppy," has a reputation with his grandchildren for having won several "most handsome man" contests. He likes to recall for them the days of World War II. Through their grandfather, they first learned of the blackouts, during which people in coastal towns and cities were expected to turn off all lights as part of the security drills in case of enemy attack.

At that time, too, Poppy worked as a shipbuilder. He tells how, owing to so many men in the armed services, American women were joining the work force to help in the war effort. He enjoys telling that he was once assigned Margie the "tacker" to work as his partner on the ship. "You're lucky she didn't become your grandmother," he once said jokingly, as he hugged his wife.

Jean, his wife of fifty-one years, a kindly woman with a warm, welcoming smile, picked up an enlarged photograph of herself that rested on the mantle. The picture, which was taken during the depression, revealed an attractive and stylish young woman, with an inner glow of acceptance. As Jean held the picture, she would unravel the secrets of that distant period. She told of her straightened circumstances, hard work, and simple joys, and she described the then current styles of women's hair and dress. She once demonstrated a popular dance step, the "Charleston." Later Jean was surprised to learn that her teenage granddaughter, Ginger, with whom she shared her reminiscences, had reported it to her social studies class as an example of life during the depression.

These grandchildren were introduced to the rudiments of what today we call hermeneutics, the science of interpretation. They learned that circumstances were continuously changing and that circumstances change understanding, but that the past is not irretrievably lost. To their delight, they saw that it is possible to make sense of the past, to learn to appreciate a very different way of thinking and acting. Assisted in the art of interpretation by the explanations of grandparents, children learn to find meaning and values in the strangest times and places, and then to recognize in their ancestors a core of life not too different from their own. They touch authentic human wisdom and goodness. Having demythologized the past, they have entered into it and made it their own. They have matured. They have broken out of the parochialism of the here and now.

Often with the arrival of the *first* grandchild, family history suddenly becomes relevant. One is motivated to put the pieces of one's life together. That's what Werner, an executive in his fifties, did after his grandchild was born. When he first learned that he would become a grandfather, he hesitated to admit it to himself. It was not time yet. All that changed, however, when the baby girl arrived. He found himself digging out old family albums that he had never had much time for. While paging through them, he rediscovered the links in the chain of family ancestors. As he reflected on each page, he began to appreciate those who had cooperated with destiny in making it possible for each succeeding generation to share in the next phase of the unfolding family line. "What would have happened," he thought, "had my own father and mother not met and married? In fact, what if my daughter had decided not to have children?" A sense of awe overtook him as he felt in his heart gratitude for the gift of life given to his new grandchild and treasured his own role and that of all his ancestors. This experience helped Werner to begin to see the pattern and plan in his own life story, which gave him a new sense of identity.

A grandparent can communicate an historical perspective to the very grandchildren whose existence has prompted the expanding of his personal horizons. Listening to stories of ancestry told by grandparents proves to be a meaningful experience for grandchildren, one that carries over into adulthood. I recall, now many years later, one late afternoon sitting across the table from my grandmother as we leisurely sipped our tea with the howling wind in the background, one voice seemed all that mattered. I was nine then, but I had no idea how old Grandma was. To me she just seemed ageless. My rapt attention signaled to her that she had captured her audience.

"When I was a child we would celebrate a wedding for a whole week. There would be much dancing and singing. Everyone had such a good time." These words were spoken in broken English by Grandma who was reliving her memories of life in Poland.

Grandma had emigrated in her youth to this country where she later met my grandfather, whom she knew from back home, married, and raised her eight children. Now she could enjoy her grandchildren. She seemed to savor especially taking me on trips through her memories and sharing reminiscences of the "old country." Not all of her stories, however, were pleasant ones. Some included tragic losses that somehow Grandma managed to survive, such as the time when her sister was shot by enemy soldiers.

As Grandma shared her stories of the past, something was happening inside me. I began to feel a sense of kinship with a faraway country, with people I had never met—except through the eyes of my grandmother. I began to imagine myself in the setting created by her and realized that, in some way, we shared a common history. Grandma was the bridge to my past; I was the bridge to her future.

Those experiences of storytelling enlarged my sense of life, of wonder, and of love. Grandma's stories connected me to people I would never know in real life. Many of them had either died or remained in Europe. Nevertheless, they had played their ancestral role in shaping my history. It turned out to be quite an adventure. I felt part of a wider family. Since then, tea-time always has been for me, thanks to Grandma, a ritual of warm feelings and story-time moments.

What makes modern grandparents so needed as historians? A significant factor, as the famous anthropologist Margaret Mead noted, is that for the last hundred years grandparents have seen more change than any other generation in the history of the world.[5] Grandparents have a long-term memory that does not decline much with age, which enables them to recall events and emotions experienced in earlier years, and to retell them in their later ones. Their memories can reach deep within a well of stored treasures to be channeled into the minds and hearts of their listeners.

Among their collectibles, grandparents have accumulated a range of stories about themselves from childhood through adulthood. Marie, an elderly but not yet retired secretary, recalls the story that her grandfather shared with her when she was a child. She enjoyed sitting on the lap of that portly old gentleman while hearing how her grandfather became a boy hero. He deftly carved out the story of the gypsies coming to his home on the farm and how he prevented them from ransacking their family's house. As the only one home, he was responsible for its security while his parents were away for the day. They had warned him in advance not to permit anyone to enter the house since they were aware of the looting being done by the gypsies in the area. When one came to the door and tried to force herself in, he slammed the door on her hand. Away she ran—along with the others.

This story and the one of how, as a young man, her grandfather had left his faraway country to come to America, helped Marie capture his spirit of daring and adventure. In telling stories of their past, grandparents can become transformed into magical figures in the eyes of a grandchild. These images carry a power of their own that can be useful resources for a child to draw upon whenever a particular need arises. A grandmother's story of how as a child she had to help support her widowed mother and siblings by leaving home and going to work in the city, can be an encouraging force for influencing a grandchild in overcoming the obstacles of life. Or the story of the grandfather, who as a young man, had made his own violin, can be an inspiration for young persons to exercise their own handicraft potentials. They feel confident that they have inherited these talents.

When adult children recall memories of a grandparent unraveling a story, they usually associate it with a particular mood and setting. A whole scene is created in one's mind that enriches the feelings and understanding. Recollection of that experience makes the grandparent, too, come alive again. The attention given to those stories as a child leads in later years to a deeper appreciation of its message and of its relevance to the present.

Psychological Overtones

Collective memory constitutes the psychological existence of a family, a group, a community, a people. Family members who share in its continuity do so through familiarity with their common story. The task of doing that falls chiefly on grandparents—those who possess long memories. The philosopher Hans Gadamer remarked that people derive their identities from the stories they tell themselves. These stories take hold within our psyche and contribute to our image of who we are and how we got that way. From family stories we learn about our personal life. We begin to understand how we fit into the family and the world. We gain clues to our present condition.

The value of this psychological process is manifest today in the family systems approach to therapy. In helping dysfunctional families, the therapist reverts to the familial story of the extended family to trace the problems and strengths that lie therein. Taking a close look at the immediate family, the grandparents, and perhaps the great-grandparents as well, often gives clues to understanding why individuals and the nuclear family behave as they do.

Family history leads to world history. Consider Alex Haley's search related in his bestselling book, *Roots*. He ventured into distant lands and a century that has long gone. He learned of strange customs and inhuman cruelty. He learned about his ancestors. But above all he learned about himself. Through his writing, he helped many others to appreciate vicariously their own heritage and to learn about themselves. The number of high school and college courses in black history shows the continuing fascination with one's roots. But this is not a purely black phenomenon; all peoples, all persons need to know their family history and heritage.

Memories begin to fade even after one generation. What happens when people forget their history? The French historian, Alexis de Tocqueville, in *Democracy in America*, reminded us of the danger, in a society such as ours, of forgetting one's roots and the dire consequences of that loss.

Democracy makes men forget their ancestors, their descendants, their contemporaries. Each man is forever thrown back on himself alone, and there is danger that he may be shut up in the solitude of his heart.[6]

Robert N. Bellah in his book, *Habits of the Heart*, makes this same point in trying to understand the moral dilemma facing contemporary American society: the conflict between fierce individualism and the need for community and commitment to others. In so concluding, he called upon the traditions that Americans can use to make sense of themselves and their society. They should look to history to understand the values that motivated earlier Americans as they built a new nation. Bellah discovered that individualism pervades American society, and that Americans have lost the language needed to make moral sense of their lives. Many today believe that in the end they are really isolated and have to answer only to themselves.[7]

An example of this psychic forlornness is the fashion king, Giorgio Armani, who rules a multimillion-dollar empire. "I feel alone, and I'm terrified," Armani said. "I'll have an eternity to be alone. I don't have many relationships with people, but at least I express myself with the clothes I design. If I didn't have that, I'd shoot myself."[8]

In counteracting tendencies toward individualism that encourage loneliness and foster a sense of alienation, a first step is to connect with one's history, to discover one's place in the larger community. Grandparents who claim their role as family historians can be important channels for enabling this understanding to occur. In relating family history as they have experienced it, grandparents reveal to the children how they came to be. This process touches their identity and tells the children their own singular story—their family origin and their development.

One example of how family history gives an historical perspective on a timely problem is the environmental crisis. There is a pressing need to save the earth from today's technological and post-industrial world devastations, where more means better and where meeting the limitless demands of a consumer society depletes natural resources and pollutes the water and air. We must make the effort to remind people that conditions were not always that way nor must inevitably be that way.

We need to recall in our imaginations the beauty of the earth in its pristine splendor—fresh air, lush forests, clean water. Grandparents possess something of that memory. Theirs is the responsibility to tell the story that connects us with our ecological heritage and that also calls for cooperation from the entire human community. Indeed, without that vision there is little hope of rescuing this planet. The future of yet unborn generations is at stake.

Spiritual Traditions

Important though our secular history is, with its sociocultural dimensions, success in fashioning our lives and remaking the world is ultimately a religious achievement. "God saw all the things that he had made and they were good" (Gen 1:31). But he gave us stewardship over the earth and willed that we grow in wisdom and grace. There is no such thing as pure nature. For all eternity God has willed to elevate human beings to a new and higher state. Human nature is graced; God's will is that all things in heaven and on earth be renewed. (see Eph 1:10).

Through storytelling, grandparents can play a decisive role in the religious formation of children by depicting for them their religious history. As living ancestors they have a special place in the family; they can make the word of God come alive for their grandchildren. Their shared mission is to communicate God's message as part of the oral tradition of the Judeo-Christian experience. These religious leaders within the family participate in the divine plan, which has existed from all eternity. Experiencing personally and concretely how that providential plan has worked in their own lives, they bear witness that those created by God in his image and likeness are loved and guided by him, whose "wisdom reaches from end to end mightily and orders all things graciously" (Wis 1:8).

Salvation history, as related in the Bible, reveals the important part that grandparents have played through cooperating with God's plan and the choice blessings bestowed upon them. The Old Testament is rich in examples.

The story of Ruth has memorable generational overtones. Elimelech and Naomi had two sons, both of whom married

Moabite women. The sons died, but one wife, Ruth, instead of staying with her own people accompanied Naomi to Bethlehem, for Ruth had accepted Yahweh as her God. Her trust in Yahweh and her fidelity to Naomi were not in vain. She married Boaz, a kinsman of Ruth's, and bore a child, named Obed. The women assured Naomi: "He shall be to you a restorer of your soul. And he will sustain you in your old age" (4:14). What restores her soul is the realization that the family name will be carried on, that the family history will continue. In fact, with a fitting metaphor, it was proclaimed: "A son is born to Naomi" (Ruth 4:17). The Talmud gave this explanation: "Ruth bore him and Naomi brought him up; hence he was called after her" (Sanhedrin 19b). That is, he was given her family name. Thus was the house of Elimelech built up, for Obed was the grandfather of David, who was an ancestor of Christ.

The story of Jacob also illustrates a similar theme, namely, that the life of a grandparent, lived in harmony with the will of God, finds continuity and fulfillment through grandchildren. Although scripture emphasized Jacob's son, Joseph, the words of Jacob's blessing are directed to his grandchildren.

> May God in whose presence my fathers Abraham and Isaac walked, may God who has been my shepherd from my birth until this day, may the angel who has been my savior from all harm, bless these boys, may my name live on in them, and the names of my fathers Abraham and Isaac, may they grow and increase on the earth (Gen 48:15-16).

Later Jacob, recalling the death of Rachel, the boy's grandmother, gained great consolation from the life of his two grandsons, Ephraim and Manasseh. Once again auspicious births have linked the past with the future. These stories also reveal how God graces nature in using family lineage as an instrument in his providential plan for all of us and how those who love him are the beneficiaries of this plan.

In the New Testament, Matthew gives attention to the

importance of the generations leading to the birth of Christ (Mat 1:1-17). In perusing the genealogical linkage of Adam and Jesus Christ, we should think of the interplay of God's providence and the free choice of human beings. How different would each family history be had any of one of countless unions been different.

Grandparents need only to ask themselves what may happen if they do not pass on their story—personal and religious—to their grandchildren. If they had no one to pass their story on to, would not the ancestral heritage come to an end, not only their family line but also their cultural and intellectual traditions? Yet, even without children and grandchildren, all remain members of the human family, and all can play a personal and intimate role in handing on the great treasures of life and religion to generations yet to come. Everyone, even in the most adverse circumstances, has the opportunity to participate in God's providential plan as it operates in personal, familial, and communal living. From eastern Europe we have a current example of this truth.

The babushka—a folded triangle of cloth tied under the chin—has long given Russian grandmothers the name "babushki." During Marxist times the practice of religion, often called "the opium of the people," was forbidden. The focus was on weaning the young from the church. Religion was left to old women. So the babushki swept the church floors, sold candles, and attended services.

Not surprisingly, these babushki also helped preserve religious continuity. Owing to them, the Christian message passed to the younger generation. For the babushki frequently lived in three generational families. One twenty-five year old Russian woman told how she was raised by her grandmother. "When my grandmother died, I was ten. I mourned as if for my mother." These extra parents were the keepers of the flame, the storytellers, and the family historians. Today many churchgoers, when asked how they learned about religion, point to their old grandmothers who whispered to them about God as they fell asleep.

The babushki now are often the only ones left in the villages as the young move to the cities. They continue to maintain the old songs and tell the old stories lest these cultural treasures be lost. Today university students are taking oral histories and preserving the stories that have been retold for generations, stories that are the seeds of the religious revival that has occurred since the breakup of the U.S.S.R.[9]

Throughout its history the Judeo-Christian family has been crucial in transmitting the religious perspective of life—its origins, meaning, and values. Grandparents are often more easily able to do so than are the parents. Owing to their wider experience, they can have deeper insights into life and have more seasoned wisdom and virtue to hand on as a spiritual heritage. Grandparents can readily be channels of religious values and meaning if they take advantage of the many opportunities to communicate creatively what they have learned so laboriously.

Grandparents can very easily explain their religious commitment at times of visits to churches and shrines as well or on holy days and festivals. Not only through the recounting of events do Judeo-Christian grandparents pass on the stories in scripture, but also through carrying out of rituals and customs. As children go through their own stages of development, grandparents can find appropriate stories and rituals to influence the child's faith development. Sacred feasts present moments of religious history: Hanukkah recalls the reconsecration of the altar of the Temple of Jerusalem that had been profaned three years before; the Christian mass itself is a ritual reenactment of the last supper and the death and resurrection of Christ.

Grandparents contribute a heightened consciousness of religion, giving these historic events a new life by embodying them in domestic practices. The grandparents, by telling the story to the children, can connect the belief to a particular moment in the life of the family. Preparing for and celebrating with the child, first communion, confirmation, bar mitzvah, Yom Kippur, Seder, Christmas dinner, May devotions, Easter, Pentecost, and All Saints' Day, can involve the grandparents in explaining these traditional ways of remembering the "great days." Since the grandparents are a generation beyond the parents, their doing these things as an ongoing part of the family's history, makes the events something special and memorable for the grandchildren—and an enduring part of their religious culture.

A Fair Exchange

To be fully productive, storytelling must be reciprocal. Through stories, grandparents finally put all the pieces of their lives together. Through stories, grandchildren start to identify the beginnings of their destiny. And turnabout is fair play.

Erik Erikson referred to the last stage of life as the "grandparental stage." This task has become identified with ego integrity, the finding of meaning and value in one's life cycle. Erikson said that this interaction enables grandparents, especially through the dynamic of storytelling, to integrate the completed and unfinished components in themselves.[10]

The verbal acts are the province of the elderly who have stories of a world and a life that have all but disappeared. They should have opportunities to tell their tales because they *enrich* us all and because, *in the telling,* the elders remember and recollect their lives. Such memories are often more vivid than recent events, perhaps because their senses were so *vitally* involved and have kept those sensory images vibrant. A long life cycle can be reviewed more effectively in this way than when it is remembered by piecemeal and by chance.[11]

Sometimes grandparents want to share stories but feel turned-off by others. When Terry, a young Washington business woman, left her house for work one morning, she noticed an elderly neighbor walking in her direction with his cane leading the way. His other hand held the leash that secured his tiny dog, Muffin. A smiling hello led to a brief conversation. She learned that he was 85 and that he had been a career diplomat and, at one time, a top political and social analyst of conditions in Spain and Portugal. In a few remarks, he clarified key aspects of the current European situation. "You're like a walking history book," she exclaimed. "You have so much to offer." "Yes," he responded, "but when you get old, nobody wants to listen." The exchange was short; but, when he walked on, his back was straighter, his step firmer.

Unfortunately, his case is not an isolated one. How do elders pass on their great knowledge of life through stories, when the young audience is reluctant to listen? Certain observations may be helpful.

Grandparents have a need to pass on their valuable wisdom and understanding of life through stories. For them it is a natural medium of exchange. They, however, need to acquire a sense of direction on just how best they can do that. They need to begin by taking into account that achieving this goal requires them to become involved in an ongoing process of storytelling, whether the grandchildren are near or far. How they do that will change as they become attuned to the needs of the developing child. Grandparents ought to become aware of the various ways they can communicate their message as well as the best means of preserving the family's story.

Because of the conflicts of schedules resulting from family mobility, divorce, and other related factors, many grandparents spend only a short time with their grandchildren. So planning in advance which stories to tell and how to tell them will maximize their opportunities, however limited. Such planning will help grandparents to guard against repetitiveness. For children tend to avoid a grandparent who sounds like a broken record. Repetition has a place, but one must wait for a child to request the story to be told again.

Another important help is the clue that the child's age gives as to what is of interest. A child of six, for example, has not developed the cognitive ability to understand distant time. This stage usually occurs at twelve or thirteen. For younger children grandparents should concentrate on stories that center on the child's own parents, not on long dead ancestors. What child is not interested in hearing about their parents when they were young? What grandparent would not enjoy recalling events of their daughter's performance in which she had the lead part, or how her daughter caused her older sister's birthday party to be a flop by accidentally dropping the cake? Grandparents have a unique opportunity to paint scenes of the grandchild's own parents and the common challenges they experienced in growing up. Sighs and laughs, discoveries and similarities emerge during these revelations.

Storytelling can be a time for strengthening emotional attachments. Even if they are unaware of it, grandparents who have a natural bond with their grandchild will communicate not just an account of events but, through their very presence, a broader intangible meaning. By doing so, the grandparent welcomes the child into a world inhabited by the ancestors who have walked the path of life long before them.

An easily overlooked point is that storytelling, to keep its audience, must be reciprocal. I realized this early.

My Grandma had, indeed, opened the door to her world by sharing life in the "old country" with me, but for some reason, she never opened the door to my childhood world, never even knocked. I would never trade those warm feelings and the sense of wonder that enveloped me during those spontaneous storytelling sessions at Grandma's house. But, perhaps a bond of greater affection would have developed between Grandma and me, had Grandma been aware of my unspoken need as a child occasionally to share my own stories with her, to start putting my pieces together.

Children have a need to connect with their grandparents, not in a superficial way, but in a manner that builds strong bonds. This type of healthy attachment assures the child of stable influences. With so many disruptive forces at work on the family and its relationships, effort is needed on the part of its members to initiate ways to strengthen it. Grandparents can profitably exercise their special role in doing this. One way is through good communication that involves not only the grand-parents as storytellers, but the grandchild as well. What can grandparents do to encourage this?

Children are often shy, and encouraging a child's narrative gifts is not always successful. Depending upon the age of a child, grandparents can begin by asking good questions of their grandchild, questions that center around topics of interest in their world. This approach will enable children to feel more comfortable and willing to share their stories.

One twelve year old grandson, Donnie, enjoys sharing stories about himself whenever his grandfather, Andy, comes to visit. When Andy discovered that his grandson was learning to make flies for fishing, he asked simply: "How did you ever become interested in that?" For the next ten minutes Donnie told of how one of his classmates once brought some flies to school and invited him to meet his instructor. Now Donnie is supplying fishing flies for his friends. Andy let his grandson do most of the talking, but would insert a remark or two to prompt further elaborations. By capitalizing on his grandson's interest, Grandpa was able to pave the way for further sharings. After listening attentively, the grandfather then shared some of his own experiences of fishing.

A question on fishing or trout streams or flies easily led Donnie to go into stories about the fellows on the trip and their problems or stories about school, sports—and later stories about girl friends and even stories he does not tell his father. Whenever they go fishing together—at least salt water fishing where silence is not so important—they swap a lot of stories.

By creating opportunities for children to tell their story, warm and memorable moments can mutually enrich both the older and younger generation. Each time one or the other shares in the event created by the storyteller, a rapport is estab-lished; a sense of the other is communicated that can lead to further eventual sharings. This openness to each other acts as a key to unlocking treasures that might otherwise remain hidden; for example, personality and character traits, particular likes and dislikes, strengths and limitations, and the special interests and expectations that each may have. Children feel secure when an adult welcomes them through attentive listening; likewise, their response makes grandparents feel needed and special. Together they establish a reciprocal audience.

Many grandparents acknowledge the feeling of an expansion of self beyond their own lifetime whenever they interact with their grandchildren. By communicating with their grandchildren they develop a unique sense of self and satisfy a need for stimulation, novelty, and fun. Storytelling is an expression of mutual giving and receiving. One tells the story, the other listens and then the roles change. This interaction also fulfills the need for altruism that the aging person often feels at this time of life. Listening–becoming a "dear ear"–can become a true act of friendship.

Getting Started

An easy way to break into storytelling is to read interesting stories to one's grandchildren. This builds the confidence to recount the equally interesting stories previously read and rehearsed alone. This method whets their appetites for stories in general and stimulates them to respond to questions such as: Did anything like that ever happen to you or your friends? What would you do if you were in that kind of a situation? Of course, the stories and the questions should be adapted to the age of the child. The right stories engender a lifetime of love for reading, which opens many doors to adventure and to wisdom.

Adlai Stevenson III, the noted statesman, benefitted from such an exposure in his early life. His paternal grandfather, the first Adlai, was a reader. Wearing a Prince Albert coat and sitting in the parlor after the Sunday noonday dinner, Grandfather Stevenson began the storytelling ritual. He would select a volume from the library and read in a deep-voiced, dramatic manner such items as Mark Antony's speech over the body of Caesar, the legend of Ichabod Crane, or the dark and bloody sections of *Hamlet* or *Macbeth*. Adlai acknowledged that it was his grandfather who aroused in him a keen interest in

American history. As a result, before he reached high school, he had read all thirteen volumes of Markham's *The Real America in Romance*. Ever after he saw his life in historical context.[12]

In addition to this historical conditioning, two major tasks are involved: collecting historical materials and preserving them. These tasks are simple but require a certain care and perseverance and may on occasion make necessary some research, such as checking baptismal records or death certificates, atlases or street maps.

Grandparents should realize that they have a view of family history that the younger generation will never share unless the grandparents make it available to them. As simple a thing as identifying the faces in a snapshot easily becomes an impossible task as members of the family die. To jot down names on the back of the snapshot together with the date and a description of the occasion takes only a moment but preserves that moment for many lifetimes.

Many other things can be collected without cluttering up the house: the family tree with names, dates, and pictures; documents, such as awards, newspaper clippings, diplomas, and even report cards; major events, secular and religious; and, finally, anything else that has special relevance to the history of the family. For example, a great treasure for younger generations would be a collection comprised of the typical expressions and jokes of each relative, their special habits, favorite foods, and choice recipes, their skills and hobbies, and whatever else made them distinct.

On a more serious note, the medical records of one's ancestors and other close relatives may shed significant light on what may as yet be undiagnosed physical and mental problems, such as tendencies toward hypertension, diabetes, atherosclerosis, or Alzheimers. In a lighter vein, records may reveal artistic, intellectual, social, religious, or comic gifts. To know that some talent is in the family or in the genes is often enough to stimulate a relative into working to realize this potential. But someone has to preserve these facts or they are forever lost.

The question then arises: how best to communicate this factual treasury of family history? Today, with all the technological aids, the difficulty is minimal: write down these facts; make a tape recording of them; or use a videocassette recorder. Let us consider each one of these methods separately.

The first and oldest method is writing. We have already suggested how the family chronicle can be made. The question is how to transmit it to the grandchildren. They will not be attracted by a list of facts, but they will be fascinated by letter stories and anecdotes. Young children especially enjoy receiving a story in the form of a letter. One grandfather who lived in another state created a story of what he did one morning beginning from the time he awoke, to his taking a walk, his interaction with people, animals, and birds along the way. Some grandparents can add a bit of drama to their accounts by having some of the birds and animals talk or telling what they think they might be saying. Children can thus pleasantly gain a clearer picture of their grandmother and grandfather. Anecdotes are especially attractive if they are short and dramatic—with a point. They easily convey a sense of values. The process itself becomes a foot in the door for still more dialogue with the youngsters as they develop.

One grandparent decided to write a play about the family. This is a good way to summarize the family's story. This medium shows what happened and who said what to whom with minimal explanation, such as detailed descriptions of scenery, personalities, and other background material. This is a good vehicle for communicating to children ten years and older.

Writing—even with a typewriter or word processor—is not for everyone. People who have worked with words—teachers, lawyers, advertisers—may enjoy this type of literary communication. Some whose work has been very different may also have a verbal skill that enables them to write easily and clearly. The telephone, however, has cut down on the practice of letter writing. Fewer people are comfortable with it, but most readily adapt to using a tape recorder or a videocassette recorder. With these helps, the possibilities are abundant. Grandparents can preserve the family story as it actually happens. Jenny, who lives in Pittsburgh, mentioned how she recorded her grandchildren's history from the time they were old enough to make sounds. At that time her grandchildren lived in the same city. "Whenever my two grandbabies were brought for a visit, I would get out the tape recorder and record their gurgles and their earliest attempts at words, such as 'mmm, mmm, dada, mamma' and one's I can't even imitate." She added, "Even as teenagers, they were fascinated by their early babbling."

As the years progressed, Jenny captured on tape the first songs sung by the grandchildren as well as many conversations between the grandchildren and their grandparents, and other relatives. On special holiday gatherings the tape recorder would appear and everyone was ready for another session with Grandma Jenny. Sometimes each member would take part in a mock performance which included an aunt, Dorothy, interviewing each of the grandchildren on some related topic. Sometimes, everyone participated in singalong sessions with a few solos in between. At other times, such as birthdays, Jenny would describe the happenings of the day in a short interview with the honoree.

Eventually the grandchildren moved to another city, but Jenny continued her taping sessions whenever she could. On occasional visits of her grandchildren, which were not as frequent as before, she would select a tape or two to play for them. She says they never tire of hearing recordings of themselves. Maybe they caught her underlying message, her way of saying, "You are very special to me. I love you all."

Tape recorders also have an advantage for grandparents who live at a distance. David, a widower who lived 375 miles from his grandchildren, decide to tape-record stories of his own childhood, poignant and meaningful ones, to share with his grandchildren. This outreach helped his grandchildren realize that their grandparents have not always been old. That they, too, had to go through the stages of childhood and learn valuable lessons, lessons that their grandfather wants to pass on to them. The children began to appreciate the many changes that have taken place since their grandparents' days. They often replay these tapes and plan someday to pass them on to their own children.

Preserving family history takes on an added dimension by combining the collection of photographs and the updating of a running commentary taped in sequence to the photographs and other important family documents such as birth records. "I enjoy spinning off anecdotes from the family photo album," expressed one creative grandparent. "It's much more interesting than just simply looking at pictures. All I do is number the pictures, get out my tape recorder, and delve into my memory bank. Some of the pictures are from a long time ago, maybe when my children were small. Others trace the varied experiences of my grandchildren during their growing years. My grandchildren enjoy it, and so do I. In reliving the cherished moments of the past, I feel uplifted and thankful for the blessings of my children and grandchildren. One day I hope that someone picks up after me and continues where I've left off."

The videocassette recorder presents a different slice of life. Making home movies when grandchildren are present is a valuable means of preserving their story. It is also an effective way to record particular moments in the life of grandparents. Videocassettes can be sent to grandchildren who might only be able to visit grandparents once or twice a year. Looking at grandparents on television enables grandchildren to enter the world of their grandparents and continue the sense of being one family.

All children need a sense of self-worth. Grandparents who choose to tell and preserve stories reminiscent of the child's past contribute to that feeling of specialness and help in the shaping of the child's identity. Grandchildren gain a sense of belonging. Likewise, a grandparent who gives loving attention to a grandchild is fulfilling his or her role as a grandparent. By collecting and recording the ongoing history of grandchildren, their writings, drawings, tape and video recordings of them, and a journal of events and experiences filling their lives, a reservoir of otherwise lost information, is preserved. This effort will reap benefits when in later years, through adult eyes, one seeks a deeper understanding of one's development and identity.

As we move into the twenty-first century, family interaction is on the decline. This interaction within the immediate and extended family plays an important role and needs to be kept alive. Enlightened grandparents try to reverse the current situation. They realize that when grandparents are out of touch, the family loses. They want to capitalize on what a prominent child psychiatrist, Dr. Arthur Kornhaber, discovered in his interviews with young people.

These children felt a natural connection between themselves and their grandparents as well as a strong need for close attachments to at least one grandparent. When that bond was broken or never acknowledged by a grandparent, the children felt wounded or incomplete, as if some vital part of themselves was missing. Children have a need for the unconditional love, nurturance, and acceptance provided by grandparents. This, according to Kornhaber, confers a natural form of social immunity on children that they cannot get from any other person or institution.[13] Storytelling fosters this kind of relationship. Through storytelling children have a direct link with their grandparents, a bond that is required for full emotional well-being.

Grandparents enjoy an advantageous position. They have time on their side to dispense wisely and creatively, through storytelling, what they have collected over time in their memory. Grandparents who tell stories and tell them well, entrust their own appropriated identity to their grandchildren, to future generations. Maybe their grandchildren will remember the stories, anecdotes, and even something of the conversations that preceded them. And perhaps certain parts of the story that have stood the test of time will be passed along for other generations to discover, explore, and celebrate God's work in their lives.

But even if they forget the details, unconsciously they will have absorbed a sense of personal identity and historical continuity enhanced by the glow of wisdom. This seasoning of young minds gives to grandparents as family historians an unending impact on the future. Done caringly and prudently, the success of their storytelling ensures that grandparents are forever.

Tips for Effective Storytelling

1. Plan ahead. Do you want to teach a lesson? Share a past or current event? Tell a humorous tale? Relate a story of distant ancestors or of the childhood experiences of their parents?

2. Be yourself. Adopt your own natural style, not preachy or dominating, not stilted or self-conscious, but caring, respectful and flexible.

3. Adapt your stories and style to the age and interests of the child. Young children enjoy stories about their parents' growing up. Older ones appreciate stories of more distant relatives, including stories about yourself and your current involvement in current events.

4. Encourage the child to share its own stories. Ask questions related to the child's interests, (e.g., hobbies, games, T.V. shows, sports, school, or friends).

5. Be an active listener. Through attention and responsiveness, and appropriate expression, show your interest in the child's story. Make suitable remarks. But let the child do most of the talking.

6. Remember that repeated stories easily become boring. This is especially so as children grow older. Wait until they request a retelling.

7. Try to be alone with the child. You want to give the child your full attention. Storytelling is the time for both grandparent and grandchild to share some part of themselves, their sensitive feelings and even their secrets.

3

GRANDPARENTS AS *MENTORS:* TEACHING SKILLS

In Homer's story of the Trojan War, we meet the wiliest of the Greek leaders, Odysseus (known to the Romans as Ulysses), the king of Ithaca and the husband of Penelope. By cleverly hiding his warriors in a wooden horse, he conquered Troy.

Before leaving for war, Odysseus entrusted his household and the care and education of his only son, Telemachus, to an old and faithful friend, Mentor. All were to obey him. Sometime after Odysseus' departure, Telemachus prayed to Athena, the patroness of Athens, whom the Greeks honored as the goddess of war, wisdom, experience, study, and handicrafts. She had sprung full grown and fully armed from the head of Zeus, combining both his wisdom and power.

As Telemachus prayed to Athena, she came to him—but with the appearance and voice of Mentor. Everafter, the word "mentor" has come to mean an enlightened and empowered person, a wise and faithful counselor. Athena, taking on the role of Mentor, lends strength both of mind and body to Mentor's undertakings. She completes what Mentor lacks by directing the young man toward new goals and ideas.

These traits, depicted in Homer's *Odyssey*, apply particularly to grandparents who assume the role of mentors. They have a reservoir of resources that younger people desperately need. With their added years, grandparents have acquired skills that they can pass on to others, together with judgments seasoned by adaptation to life's many changes. In sharing their skills and their practical reason with the younger generation, they can fulfil their role as mentors. In doing so, they perfect themselves as nurturers, for mentoring is a practical extension of love and concern.

An Encompassing Task

Grandparents as mentors make a commitment of friendship and trust. Building on this personal foundation, they use wisdom, talents, and skills to facilitate full development. Grandparents are also practical guides in helping a new generation to avoid life's pitfalls, in enabling them to envisage good opportunities and creative ways of doing things, and in patiently standing by while they take up the challenges for which the mentor has prepared them. What the mentor shares will enhance a young person's life by fashioning reasonable expectations that can look forward to solid accomplishments.

The grandparent mentor helps to draw forth from the child its special gifts, talents, and abilities. Sometimes this calls for giving detailed instruction in introducing the young one to new ways of doing things. At other times, a mentor may merely point out the range of possibilities or encourage one to discover on his own how to do something or how to solve a problem. During this process, the grandparent stands by as a patient observer—willing to help, but only if necessary.

In guiding a young person a mentor must weigh things carefully to discern just exactly when and how much she is able to handle on her own; when to step aside and let her take the lead; when to advise her on the next step to be taken; and what and how much to instruct her. Should circumstances arise for new learning, a mentor will know how to assist in a beneficial way.

As mentors, grandparents are involved in a complex relationship, which is more than merely conveying knowledge and passing on life skills. A teacher on television can do that much and yet not be a mentor. Rather, mentoring involves a mutual relationship that has been cultivated over time, one which is fused with the personal interest of the mentor and aimed at the well-being of the younger person. A mentor offers herself, her presence, along with her knowledge and know-how for the good of the grandchild. This presence is an inviting one, open, loving, encouraging, respectful—qualities of a nurturer—that enables the grandchild to feel secure and accepted: "I'm OK." As nurturers, grandparents have already begun to lay the foundation for teaching and offering sound advice to grandchildren. Mentoring is, as we have said, a practical extension of nurturing.

Grandparent mentors, relating as nurturers, foster the development of a bond of trust between themselves and their grandchildren. Such a bond underlies a mentor's relationship with a grandchild, and reassures the young person that she can always count on her grandparent no matter what. A mentor remains faithful to this expectation by doing whatever is reasonably necessary to achieve this quality. Ongoing support for a grandchild is another essential ingredient for a nurturing mentor relationship. The trust reinforces a grandchild's ability to be a faithful friend.

Grandparents have a head start in teaching about the past. Their inside knowledge of family history provides fuel for children in their quest to learn about matters close to home. Grandchildren are then able to broaden their understanding as to who they are and, depending upon their age and development, to gain insight into their own tendencies, talents, and interests, and to discover the connection between that and their living and deceased ancestors. These grandparent mentors can also draw from their storehouse of memories what can be valuable in helping children gain a sense of the past and the many rapid changes that have occurred during their lifetime. Sharing history is an extension of mentoring by showing what has been done and what can be done.

Archbishop Patrick Flores of San Antonio, Texas, remembers how his Hispanic grandparents influenced him through the sharing of history. While his parents worked picking vegetables in the fields, young Patrick's grandparents solicitously cared for him. Listening to his grandfather re-create stories of the Mexican outlaw, Pancho Villa, was one way he learned about the history of Mexico. His grandmother, however, would tell him religious stories of Jesus. To her he credits his religious formation which later culminated in his call to the priesthood. She gave him the confidence to take so great a step.

As mentors, grandparents can relate to younger generations both within the family as well as outside it. Young children, with their sense of wonder and curiosity, stand ever-ready for a grandmother or grandfather to teach them something new, or to help them improve upon what they already know.

On the other hand, adolescents have different needs because of their developmental stage. They need a caring person to help them move successfully into adulthood. Yet their opportunities to establish meaningful relationships with adults may be limited due to family fragmentation, age-segregation in school, or geographic mobility which hinders them from establishing much needed roots.

Youths who find themselves at risk are often disconnected from family, work, community, and the future. But they are all too familiar with isolation, a sense of powerlessness and low self-esteem. Help is crucial during this phase of development. Having a good mentor can mean learning how to cope and survive and build new skills and self-reliance to enrich one's life. A good mentor can buffer the stresses of adolescence.

Many grandparents help young people in classroom settings, ranging from day-care centers to the university. Former Secretary of Education, Lamar Alexander, stressed the important role of grandparents by expressly putting older citizens at the forefront of his drive to reform education. Alexander stated that most grandparents would be frightened into action if they saw how children spend a day or what they watch on television. "I think an older American who is a grandparent will want to help children change the way our children are growing up and help them learn more." Grandparents, he insisted, should do whatever they can to ensure that children enter school ready to learn. His closing remarks emphasized this point:

> With your own grandchildren, you can hug them, listen to them, read to them, play with them, take time with them, let them grow up knowing that someone is crazy about them and expects them to succeed. That's the most important thing.[1]

More and more, we hear the expression that he or she is my mentor. In the autobiography of Woody Herman, *The Woodchopper's Ball*, he pays tribute to his high-school teacher and mentor, Sister Fabian Reilly, O.P. Sister Fabian was someone on whom Woody could count, not just for instruction, but for the interest she took in him. She believed in him and recognized his talent as a jazz musician. In his description of his student/mentor relationship, Woody gives us some clues as to what a lasting influence this had.

According to Woody, he was always a little behind in his work because of his musical activities. Whenever he was sent to the principal's office, Sister Fabian always arrived first to "cop a plea for him." Whatever the problem, she would help him work it out. "Just stick to your music," she would say. "It's the best thing for you. You'll learn the other things."

Sister Fabian continued to support and save him all through his high school days. As Woody moved on in life he managed to correspond for years with Sister Fabian. And, whenever he came to town, he met with her. While achieving success as a band leader, he never forgot Sister Fabian. At least once a year he tried to perform for his former high school—his way of paying tribute to his mentor.[2]

Untapped Powers

Maude Perry had been elected president of the Variety Club at the Asbury Methodist Home in Gaithersburg,

Maryland, and was responsible for planning programs for about ninety elders in the senior resident's home where she lives. In her letter to me she requested that I address their group on "The Value of Senior Citizens in This Modern World." Maude said that she would like the talk to be a build-up. What good are we? What can we do? How can we help? She finds that now so many older people feel they have nothing to offer. They feel useless. Nevertheless, she believes that each person has a talent and that there is a need to reverse the attitude that many elders themselves share as a result of the prevailing ageism, discrimination on the basis of chronological age.

Maude's questions touch the critical issue of the meaning of life. The struggle for answers to these questions comes from the vital need to be involved with life. Eighty-eight year old Viktor Frankl, M.D., Ph.D., professor of neurology and psychiatry at the University of Vienna Medical School in Austria, and survivor of Auschwitz, insisted on the need to find meaning in life. For life to be filled with meaning, one must transcend oneself and become involved with others. Life in and of itself has unconditional meaning which can be found by each and every person regardless of sex or age, intelligence or educational background, environment or character, or even religious commitment.

But if unconditional meaning and value are immanent in life, why do so many elders fail to realize this truth? After having lived relatively long lives, should they not have somehow arrived at this conclusion themselves?

A partial explanation for the emptiness in the lives of many elders is their failure to forget themselves and to love others. The remedy requires the breaking out of the self-centered attitude that manifests itself in narcissistic behavior, whereby a "me first" policy plays a decisive role in one's choices. Such a mindset reveals an attempt at an obligation-free approach to the demands of family, friends, society (including its institutions), and the environment.

Why do elders now find themselves searching for meaning, lacking obligation, feeling isolated and inferior? What role has society in contributing to this mentality?

An article in *U.S. News & World Report* entitled "America's Forgotten Resource: Grandparents," emphasized the rapid social changes in recent decades that have combined to threaten a most important resource of American families—the grandparents. With the increase in divorce and mobility, grandparents and grandchildren have been separated. Some grandparents, however, have purposely played a part in this estrangement. They have chosen a life apart, given over to outside employment, to travel, or to pure leisure. Yet elders have other personally compelling needs. "They need to find more ways by which they can share their skills and perspectives," says Dr. Donald Conroy of the National Institute for the Family.[3]

Grandparents are sensitive to the negative consequences of social change affecting their role in the family. Institutions and surrogates are replacing them. At one time they helped with family needs and decision making. They handed on the family's values and traditions—ensuring continuity and connectedness. Now, they are no longer being sought out for their experience of life and their good counsel, their help in child rearing, their stories, their talents, and their skills. Their lack of contact is further reinforced by age segregation on all levels of society.

Modern life has been aptly described by Richard Bolles as a journey through three boxes. First we get an education, then we find employment, and finally we reach retirement.[4] From that point on our life is downhill—so we are led to believe. After retirement there does not seem to be anything left to which we can put our minds and talents. No longer economically productive, we are held to be personally of little or no value.

Furthermore, our consumer philosophy promotes policies that are subtly transferred to all other aspects of life. What is old is disposable or useless. If it does not work anymore, throw it out. Youth is the ideal. Age needs to be concealed and forgotten.

This present societal condition must be challenged. Grandparents themselves can take the lead in reversing the inversion of values that is proving so destructive in our society. They need to nudge one another to take a good look at themselves to discover their own abilities and attributes. As Maude Perry said, "Everyone has at least one talent." And much good—and personal joy—can come from even one talent.

Perhaps a good place to begin is where grandparents find themselves. Grandparents whose talents have been focused in a particular career or vocational trade might begin by discovering what job skills they can easily pass on to their grandchild. Others might take into account whatever it is they do best or whatever they most enjoy doing.

The possibilities abound. For example, there are grandparents who are or have been mechanics, artists, hairdressers, accountants, lawyers, singers, gardeners, fishermen, policemen, firemen, athletes, carpenters, linguists, teachers, politicians, bakers, nurses, Ph.D.s, environmentalists, researchers, musicians, farmers, magicians, social activists, writers, volunteers—their roles are legion.

Why not pass on the torch to a younger person? Grandad Marlin, for example, always enjoyed playing a good game of golf. Whenever his grandson, Peter, would come to town for a visit, Grandad would take Peter golfing. Over the years he was able to help Peter sharpen his skills. Later, when Peter became an industrial executive, he felt confident in taking prospective clients golfing. His success with his clients, he admits, owes much to the golfing expertise he learned from his grandfather. Thanks to his grandfather's great skill, Peter always plays a good game of golf, and thanks to his grandfather's gracious manners, he sometimes discreetly misses a putt.

Jim Wood, who is a soft spoken fifty-five year old grandfather of three young grandsons, has a real sense of concern for passing on something of his accomplishments to them. The seeds for doing so were planted by both his grandfathers who, in different ways, were mentors to him.

Jim, now a long-time resident of Gaithersburg, Maryland, often recalls the enriching experiences he had as a child, both in the Adirondack mountains of New York and in New

Hampshire. It was these, Jim feels, that reinforced his entrepreneurial tendencies.

When he was about eight years old, he started helping his Grandfather Wood to make candy in his two-storied red brick candy factory in Concord, New Hampshire. He would do this during his visits there. The candy factory had a place for everyone: aunts, uncles, and cousins. The grandchildren had the job of jamming the sticks into the hot pliable candy before the fan cooled it down. Jim remembers how Alvin Wood's four-inch lollipops became popular. Because of their unique size, they became known as "Longfellow lollipops."

Grandfather Wood also had a large garden and a strawberry patch. He would pay five cents a basket to each grandchild who was ambitious enough to take up the challenge of picking. "Grandpa must have had a secret," remarked Jim. "His strawberries were huge. Twelve of them filled a basket to overflowing!" From his grandfather Jim learned to appreciate the rewards of his labor—strawberries included!

Jim's maternal grandfather, Robert Schufelt, had a farm. During the wintertime Jim recalls participating in the gathering of the maple syrup from the buckets that hung from the trees. Jim often delights in reminiscing about the changes his grandfather initiated in facilitating the transport of sap from the trees to the sugar house where it was cooked. Instead of using horses to pull the vats up the mountains, his grandfather installed pipes which were connected to the sugar house. All the children had to do was to pour the sap into the pipes at the top of the hill, and down it went into the sugar house!

His busy grandfather took time to teach him how to milk cows while sitting on a one-legged stool. "Grandfather had mastered the skill of being able to tip it in any direction and keep his balance while milking cows," he said. This grandfather introduced him to plants as yet unfamiliar, such as rhubarb. To this day, when the season arrives, Jim must have his rhubarb pie.

Sandwiched in-between two enterprising grandfathers who provided an opportunity for their grandchildren to learn new skills, left its mark on Jim Wood. Although not a farmer or candy maker, Jim has learned not to hide his talents. As his grandfathers before him did, he plans to pass on some of his skills, especially in carpentry, to his own grandchildren.

No one knows better than Baltimore Orioles' pitcher Mike Kendall Flanagan what is owed to a grandfather mentor, Edward Flanagan.[5] This Manchester, New Hampshire, boy knew that "a knock on the door by his grandfather meant an invitation to play catch." By that time his grandfather was in his late sixties and a legend in his own right. He had started in 1913 with the Boston Red Sox—then a minor league team—and could pitch either right-handed or left-handed with equal force and accuracy. He often switched hands in doubleheaders and was no less adept as an ambidextrous hitter or outfielder.

Mike said that playing with his grandfather taught him good control. As a starting pitcher with the Baltimore Orioles, and famous for his landslide win of the Cy Young Award in 1979, he remembers the measures his grandfather took to teach him. When the boy's throw to him was not good, he would make him chase the ball. He had to make good throws if he did not want to get exhausted.

Grandfather Flanagan's parents had come over during the potato famine in Ireland and had no money. He built his house by hand, never had a mortgage, and never had any other debts. That did not surprise Mike who says that he never knew anyone more self-sufficient.

Mike closely watched his grandfather. Woodworking, which was his grandfather's hobby, eventually became his own hobby. Mike says that there is no end to what he had learned from his grandfather about baseball—"right down to that slippery elm was the best substance for throwing those illegal spitballs."

Whatever their talents, whatever their skills, whatever their knowledge, grandparents can tap into them and share then with the younger generation. Even when it comes to many of the little things that we take for granted, such as teaching a child to shake a bottle well before opening it, or how to tie a double knot on lengthy shoe strings, mentoring grandparents can often supplement instructions that busy parents may over-look. Consider what enriching experience grandparent mentors can add to a young person's life! We need grandparents who care enough to do their part in shaping the future. The ones who do, the regenerative ones, can make a difference in the lives of others as well as in their own.

Overcoming Obstacles

In his 1990 inaugural address the new president of the American Association of Retired Persons (AARP), Robert Maxwell, called upon older Americans to make a difference in the lives of youth, in the lives of their contemporaries, and in their own lives. He challenged grandparents to share their wisdom, skills, and values. "We can use our resources to help youngsters and at the same time, enrich our lives as well," he counseled. Enrichment means the discovery of new meaning and value.

One of the paradoxes of life is that when we give of our-selves we become more ourselves. We gradually learn who we really are. By giving to another, of our time, energy, talents, and loving presence, we go beyond the boundaries of the ego and are able to identify with a higher purpose. Throughout life our common vocation is to become more fully human through giving of ourselves.

Yet many good-willed grandparents face impediments, real or imagined, that prevent them from becoming actively involved as mentors. As much as they might feel in their hearts a desire to pass on their accrued knowledge, sound advice, experience, and skill, something seems to be standing in the way. What can they do about it?

First of all, grandparents need to identify the particular obstacles confronting them; and secondly, they need to decide creatively the best way to overcome them. Finally, they need to take action. These obstacles may stem from society in general or from one's family or one's self.

We have already considered the influence of society in fostering ageism and in promoting a youth culture. Those trends do affect the way grandparents see themselves—inadequate because of aging or unneeded by today's younger generations.

In addition, the educational system does not integrate the whole life process of maturation, parenthood, and aging with the individual differences in temperament and constitution that influence our general perspective of life. So each elder generation gets left behind while the younger generation still learns an imperfect version of the life process.

Our society's educational policy has been to educate the next—the new generation—and to set aside the older generation in the hope that, as older men and women are passed over, their outmoded forms of knowledge will do no harm. In the end, all generations lose out.

As a result, in particular, grandparents, who have lived decades longer than the younger generation and thus possess a wider perspective of life and survival, receive little encouragement and opportunity to put their special abilities to work. Without a solid educational policy that includes the older population's input and without backing from society, elders either succumb to the general malaise on this issue, begin to ignore their own skills and experiences, or simply do not realize what they have to offer young people. Over time, grandparents themselves can become immersed in this mind set. In unwittingly accepting these conditions, they become promoters of a philosophy of disengagement that limits the use of their full potential in being of service to others.

Sometimes one's own family circumstances discourage a mentoring relationship between grandparents and the other generations. Distance, too, is a factor in making contact with grandchildren. Furthermore, the grandchild's parents might make little effort in promoting a friendly relationship with grandparents.

Personal obstacles the grandparents will easily identify. Poor health certainly cuts down on the amount of time to be spent with a younger person. Certain physical impairments hamper the amount and kind of activities. Being uninformed about young people of various ages and about how to relate to them, are road blocks for grandparents interested in fostering a mentor relationship with grandchildren.

From a positive perspective, grandparents need to believe in themselves and to encourage and support other grandparents in sharing their talents, skills, and knowledge. Their effort has the long-range effect of recruiting future grandparents to mentor. Those already mentoring feel empowered by connecting with others of a like-mind.

Often grandparents cannot wait for the children's parents to take the lead in suggesting a time and place that they can share with their grandchildren. Taking the initiative, grandparents can share family and cultural history, including their own personal experiences, through storytelling and letter writing. By consistently being in contact with their grandchildren by telephone, through correspondence, or in person, grandparents can discuss current events while discovering the views of young people. This kind of relating helps bridge the gap created by distance as both learn from one another.

An enthusiastic grandparent can also whet a grandchild's appetite for learning a practical skill by mailing a sample of something she has made and by promising to teach that particular skill on her next visit. This strategy can add to the excitement of an eager-to-learn grandchild. And whenever the two meet, their secret pact will open the door to spontaneous communication.

Sometimes working at a hobby in the presence of the grandchild will prompt the child to ask how to do it. Grandparents should respond wholeheartedly. At times, the grandparent, recognizing a grandchild's skill, might ask the child's help. Learning together fosters the relationship and encourages further opportunities for learning. Adopting one or other of these approaches leads to other mutual learning experiences.

How one proceeds in a mentor-learner relationship depends largely on the age or developmental level of the grandchild. Grandparents who need help in understanding the stages of development of young people can get some help from a library. Librarians are a willing and creative resource. Updated information on child development can be found there and in local book stores. If need be, grandparents might even take workshops to enhance their skills. Grandparents who challenge themselves to learn about today's youth will be able to communicate more fully and effectively while mentoring.

One way of becoming more involved as a mentor is to be on the lookout for special talents and gifts in the young person and to encourage their use. That happened to two-time Pulitzer Prize winner and scientist, E.O. Wilson of Harvard University. His sixth-grade teacher noticed his talent in writing about birds and animals. From that point on she headed him in the direction of science. So, for example, his fascinating study of ants, seems in retrospect to be the product of a youthful interest fostered by a perceptive teacher. But not just school teachers, but grandparents, too, can have a role in identifying and encouraging the use of a young person's gifts and talents.

Grandparents find religious occasions as special times for mentoring. Whether it be Easter, Passover, High Holydays, the child's patron saint's day or visits to churches or shrines, the grandparent can explore with the child its religious message. Religious symbols such as the cross, menorah, statues, the Easter candle, and sacramentals can be introduced and explained. Catholics grandparents could even teach the child how to pray the rosary and use the occasion to teach about the main events in the life of Christ. Jewish grandparents can teach the Shema and pray with their grandchildren from the siddur (prayer book) selected prayers for special occasions.

Most important, grandparents can teach grandchildren to have a sense of God's presence and action in their lives. Talking one-to-one with a grandchild about the goodness of God and his special care for all, while mentioning how God has worked in their own life, teaches a grandchild about God's providence— God's loving care for human destiny despite the prevalence of evil in the world. In the presence of their grandchild they should feel comfortable in praying aloud short, spontaneous prayers. Their example makes God's presence more real to the child. A child who learns to live with God in his mind and in his heart, has mastered the greatest of all lessons. Grandparents can play a major role in fostering the spiritual development of their grandchildren.

What about those elders who do not have their own grandchildren or who meet with insurmountable obstacles for mentoring their grandchildren? They, too, can become involved with young people. Their neighborhood, local school, day-care center or recreational center is a good place to begin making contacts. Starting friendly conversations with young persons who live nearby can foster a relationship that may lead to mentoring. In some instances many retired elders are becoming active mentors in local universities, directing their expertise and professional skills in helping young adults establish themselves in the same field.

Visiting the children's ward in a hospital affords a valuable opportunity for mentoring. One unmarried, middle-aged man, Leonard Suza, who works for the federal government in Washington, D.C., pays a weekly visit to Children's Hospital. There he reads to children and tells them stories. He says he receives a great deal of satisfaction from his encounters with the sick children he helps, especially from those who receive no visitors. "That happy look on their face when I'm with them," he said, "makes it all worthwhile."

Grandparents benefit from mentoring. Old age, as Erik Erikson says, requires interdependence coupled with "generativity"—transmitting one's knowledge and experience to another generation, whether related biologically or psychologically. Grandparents are in an ideal position to assume the role of mentor. Unlike professionals and parents, they have great flexibility in providing ongoing support and in establishing genuine, mutually beneficial relationships with young persons to satisfy their need for generativity. Grandparents do not have to wait for their biological clock to signal when to begin. Where there are young people, there is always the opportunity for a grandparent—as a wise counselor, a friend, or a teacher—to respond.

In the long run society as a whole will benefit. By mentoring the younger generation, grandparents will be sending out a positive message to others. Instead of being classified as "takers" from the coffers of society, grandparents will be creating a new image of themselves as "givers." In doing so, they reverse their current image as victims and passive observers and become active agents of change. Reaching out to the younger members—children, youth, and even young adults—will call for a like response from their beneficiaries, either now or in the future. Grandparents will thereby prepare their own grandchildren to be mentors themselves.

The On-site Training

Opportunities abound for grandparents to become mentors. But where do grandparents begin? Wherever they find themselves to be. Usually that means within the family. Grandparents who have missed past opportunities to become vitally involved with their grandchildren can begin making a breakthrough by seizing the teaching/guiding moments that open up new doors. In the process, grandparents can often become learners, too, making new discoveries and at the same time energizing themselves. Bob Kasey understands what that means.

While on vacation at a beach resort with his family, which included his three young granddaughters, Bob decided one afternoon to walk to the local library. Finding it closed they disappointedly turned away and walked in the direction of the town hall. Just as they passed by Bob decided to look around. The children agreed. Upon entering, they met four friendly policemen. Bob mentioned their interest in finding out what went on in the town hall. Immediately the officer began explaining to the children: "If you ever get lost, come back here and find officer Joe, because he gives lost children cokes and candy and finds their parents."

After hearing this good news, the children met with Michelle, the meter reader. They learned about her job and were cautioned about keeping the parking regulations, which she said she strictly enforced.

Then Bob got permission to go into the administrative offices where three ladies described the function of their office and the responsibilities there. In terms the children could understand, they explained about their job of collecting money and paying bills.

Suddenly, much to their surprise, the fire siren blasted a deafening call which led to a live dramatization of volunteer firemen speeding to the station and jumping onto trucks. Meanwhile the policemen scrambled into their cars and sped away. As Bob and his granddaughters walked around the fire station, the shrill pulsating whistle of the rescue van jolted them. Finally, calming down, they decided to get back to their original plan for a walk on the boardwalk.

The next afternoon Bob and his granddaughters returned to the town hall to see the policemen who worked the evening shift. They soon discovered whom to look for in case they got lost in the evening.

Because of the rain on the following Sunday, Bob decided to try an experiment. He gathered his granddaughters together and asked them what they had remembered about their visit to the town hall. As they reminisced, he wrote their story on a large pad. One of the granddaughters added several lines at the bottom of the pad explaining how the story was dictated to Grandpa. The feeling of togetherness delighted them all. Later they insisted that the members of the family read the report and talk about it.

In the end Bob had to admit that he discovered how valuable it was to experience something directly instead of merely reading or being told about it. Bob finds that he often gets unexpected benefits when he pays attention to his intuitions and impulses. Moreover, what may seem mundane or obvious to adults can be a powerful and positive learning experience for children. Bob knows the secret—to seize the opportunity in the present moment. His advice to grandparents is: "Stay on your toes!"

When I had first met Bob he shared his "conversion" story with me. "Two years ago, I wasn't the same as I am today. Having just retired I was not sure how to use my energy productively," recalled Bob. After much struggle and a great deal of reflection, he emerged from his depression realizing he cared most about his family. In becoming vitally involved with his own grandchildren, Bob unleashed his bottled-up energy and found a new sense of purpose. He discovered what it means to be a creative grandparent and has now dedicated himself to spreading the message to other grandparents. By founding a national organization, "Creative Grandparenting," which sponsors a newsletter and workshops, Bob encourages others to make similar discoveries.[6]

Like Bob Kasey, grandparents who take the initiative in helping children to respond to new learning opportunities will be guiding them to thresholds of new knowledge. Moreover, grandparents, in doing so, can tap into their own skills. Their expertise resulted from having confronted life and its many unexpected challenges. Some of them related to survival, others to enrichment. Over the years the elder generation has had time to sharpen them. Unfortunately, a number of their skills may be lost to future generations if they are not passed on. Virginia, a middle-aged woman from Pennsylvania, had such an experience.

Virginia's grandmother found herself widowed at the age of thirty-two. Because she lived at the time when there was no public assistance available, she had to discover creative ways of helping her family of six children survive. One way she did so was as a seamstress. Grandmother Caroline, called "Babcia" by her grandchildren, knew how to design clothing and make dress patterns—a skill she had learned as a young girl before coming to America to raise a family. Babcia's talents, which were many, also lay in creatively designing and making stuffed animals and dolls. In addition, she crocheted the beautiful doilies used to grace her small lamp tables and dresser. Looking back, Virginia sadly wonders why Babcia never taught her those skills that were second nature to her. Being a shy child she lacked the courage to ask Babcia to teach her. Now she wishes her grandmother had only thought to pass on those valuable techniques. They died with her.

Other grandparents do not wait for children to ask them how to do something. They take the initiative and begin as soon as the child seems ready, to lay the foundation for teaching skills that require much time and preparation. One such talent is painting.

Susan Lapinski, a writer in New York and the mother of two children, describes how her husband's mother, a portrait painter, has taught seven year old Jessica. The grandmother set up a little easel for Jessica beside the big one in her studio. Her remarks—"How did you ever sketch that elephant in three strokes? I could never do that!"—were made to help Jessica gain the confidence and patience that would enable her to learn the rudiments of painting. When the child has difficulties she is told the secret: to look slowly, carefully, and simply paint what she sees, not what she thinks. With this simple coaching, the budding artist in on her way.

Creative grandparents try to make the most of teachable moments in sharing what they know best. One medical doctor shows his granddaughter how to use his big microscope when she visits. Afterwards he sends her slides for her own smaller microscope. That experience reinforces what he has taught her. Knowing that both have something special to share strengthens their bonds.

Gerry Leubner, from Rochester, New York, enjoys a variety of interests and talents. Although his grandchildren live in Texas, California, and New Hampshire, that does not discourage him from imparting his knowledge and skills to them. One summer, his ten year old grandson, Eric, came to spend several weeks with Gerry and his wife, Rita. Gerry was then involved in an archaeological dig sponsored by the Rochester Museum. The dig, a several hour drive from his home, involved six weeks of on-site camping. One weekend, Rita took young Eric to see what his retired grandfather was doing. Soon after they had arrived, Gerry was busy showing Eric how to do some of the steps involved in the process of finding small pieces of artifacts that would give clues to the inhabitants of that area. Eric soon made up his mind that when old enough he would work in a dig with his grandfather.

When another grandson visited the Leubners, Gerry was building a model of the village and house where Martin Luther had lived in Germany. As the youngster intently observed his grandfather, his interest and desire grew into an enthusiastic: "Grandpa, can I help?" The work was tedious. Nonetheless, both contributed to its completion. What a lesson in patience, perseverance, and skill had this grandson learned. The boy's sense of accomplishment and satisfaction could be seen in his face when they displayed the model to the other family members. Without realizing it, the child was learning about his own religious heritage.

In a mentor relationship a grandparent figure can interact with the younger generation even if they are not biologically related. These mentors may be older persons who have never had children or grandchildren. For example, celibate priests and sisters who sometimes overlook their potential because they have no immediate family or because they are in a retirement home with little opportunity to be with younger people. Nonetheless, their lives can be enriched if they are alerted to the fact that they, too, possess important skills and knowledge that could be of benefit to the younger generation or that might be lost if not transmitted to others.

Ninety year old Sister Mathia who had been a gifted teacher in her day but was now retired from active duty, discovered her role as a grandparent mentor. Thanks to the insight of the principal of the private school which shared the building where she resided, Sister Mathia was able to renew her love for children in a creative way. Rather than be apart from children since her retirement after over fifty years of teaching, Sister Mathia joyfully accepted the invitation to teach one of the special classes that would meet for one period every Friday. What was her special skill? Knitting. Each week the children who chose to be in her group eagerly awaited her presence. The love and patience that she engendered was an added bonus. In the meantime, throughout the week, children could be seen walking through the halls carrying their knitting bags and sneaking in a few stitches whenever there was an extra moment. What pride there was when they completed their knitting project! Sister had passed on her skill—and along with it, her love. Perhaps one day those children, as grandparents, will do likewise.

Grandparent mentors have many advantages in sharing their know-how with the younger generation. If the relationship is characterized by unconditional love, already a basic trust has been established between old and young, which leads to a positive learning environment. This secure relationship frees the child's creative energies, and affords a fun-filled atmosphere of mutual exchange. Both grandparents and grandchildren can gain from one another.

Environmental Alertness

Mabel and her teenage granddaughter had always enjoyed each other's company. Unlike some grandchildren who, when they reach their teen years seem to drift apart from grandparents, Holly has always been close to hers.

One day during a visit from Holly, Mabel mentioned the current environmental crisis and asked what the high school was doing about it. Mabel then sought her granddaughter's views about the huge amount of waste that is creating monumental problems for the planet. Holly's interest grew strong as she talked with her grandmother. Before long, Mabel suggested that they both watch the five-part T.V. series, "Race to Save the Planet." This series provoked further discussion, and finally Mabel and Holly decided on a common project. Since the issue of waste had initially stirred their interest and because their discussions of the series made them more aware of their environmental responsibilities, they agreed to do something that would cut down on waste in their lives. At first, this task seemed too tall an order. But they decided to take a step-by-step approach on reducing this problem in their lives.

Mabel and her granddaughter began by taking an "environmental walk" through Mabel's house. They listed all the devices connected with the energy sources of water, light, and heat. Holly found this to be a lot of fun. Moving from room to room she listed: refrigerator, water faucets, dishwasher, shower, stove, water heater, air conditioners, and lamps. Grandma's list was about the same but with the addition of the car which was parked in her garage.

After they compared notes, they decided to consider each device and try to think up ways to save energy. Mabel recalled her childhood days when her parents had trained her sisters and her to turn off the faucet while brushing their teeth. Holly concluded that running water unnecessarily is truly wasteful, especially when they considered people is such places as Africa and India who had very little of it and even California which was at the time, experiencing a five-year shortage. "I guess we have been using more than our share," commented Holly.

Holly's eagerness to move on to the next item listed on her paper added to Mabel's enthusiasm. She, however, thought it might be better to concentrate on only a few devices at a time. Together they decided that when they completed their project, they would call a family meeting and present this as a conservation project for everyone to participate in—adding their ideas as well. Doing this project with her granddaughter gave Mabel the opportunity to share her own "home remedies" for conserving natural resources such as water and energy. But she garnered some new insights from Holly.

Grandparents have much to teach the younger generation on how to care for the environment. Many grandparents who lived during the depression years were forced to discover ways of conserving, reusing, and recycling what they already had. Sherman Morrison, a young man in his twenties and presently living in Washington, D.C., while chatting with his maternal grandmother who lives in western Pennsylvania, discovered the values that she and her family integrated into their lives on the farm. He remembers his grandmother's words vividly: "We wanted nothing. We saved everything. We made do with what we had." Inspired by her philosophy, Sherman now works full-time for the North American Coalition on Religion and Ecology.

Grandparents, however, should enhance their knowledge and understanding of present environmental conditions that need immediate attention if the planet is to survive. As Carl Sagan and other scientists have warned, we may have about ten years to reverse the ill effects on planet earth. Given this reality, what can grandparent mentors do about it? Here is how some grandparents confronted specific environmental issues and challenges.

A grandfather who lived with his family in an area where there was a toxic waste dump realized that he did not grasp its full implications. In his day he had never even heard of toxic dumps. Now a critical issue faced his family and neighborhood. He decided to take action and learn what he could about it. He began by researching information in the local library. Next, he wrote to particular environmental organizations for more information. Whenever his grandchildren and children would open up the topic for discussion, he was well equipped to offer reasonable explanations to their questions. By making an effort to gain new knowledge through a deeper understanding of an environmental problem, and by sharing that with members of the younger generation, this grandfather proved to be a helpful mentor as well as a responsible family leader. Very soon two of his older grandchildren joined him and formed an environmental club at their school. He was the first speaker invited.

Everyday life presents many opportunities for grandparents to demonstrate ways children can do their part in improving the environment. Without sounding preachy, grandparents can lead into a conversation with the younger generation by asking questions related to environmental concerns. They can then look for opportunities to pull from their own storehouse of memories specific knowledge and practical solutions to current problems.

If the concern, for example, relates to the use of energy and the depletion of fossil fuels, a grandparent can share a story of their childhood days when there were no refrigerators. Their homes depended on iceboxes. In the icebox was a big block of ice that kept the food cold. Eventually, though, the ice would melt and had to be replaced each week by the ice man. This was nearly not as convenient as it is now. But it did not use up the earth's resources as refrigerators do.

It would be hard to convince us to give up refrigerators today. Modern grandparents must connect the so-called, outdated practices (for the conservation of energy), with an updated approach. By asking a grandchild what they think happens each time they open the refrigerator door might elicit a guess about the amount of cold air that escapes. Grandparents could tell them that each person opens the refrigerator door about twenty-two times a day or over eight thousand times a year. Unfortunately, what happens when you open the door is that the cold air rushes out, trading places with the hot air rushing in. As a result, it takes more electricity to cool the air once again.

Grandparents can enlarge upon the concept of energy and refrigeration as the exchange of information continues. "Did you know," they might add, "that when a refrigerator is full of food it needs less energy to keep cold, because the food takes on the lower temperature and keeps it trapped inside?"

The grandparent can then point out the inside dial in the refrigerator and explain that it is used for adjusting the temperature. (Many people do not know this, and so the refrigerator often winds up colder than it needs to be.) The dial should be set between thirty-eight degrees and forty-two degrees. If it is a little higher, the food will stay cold with less electricity. If the food feels icy, the dial needs to be raised.

Moving on in the conversation, grandparents can point out the coils—the things that look like tubes—that are on the back or bottom of the refrigerator. Why are they so important? Because they help keep the refrigerator cold by taking the heat out from the inside. They don't work well, however, when they are dusty.

After an interesting discussion with the grandchild, a grandparent can help to reinforce these concepts by encouraging the child to decide what they can do in conserving energy while using the refrigerator. Perhaps the grandparent and grandchild could try a joint project together—such as each one keeping a record of how many times they open the refrigerator during the day. And how long does each keep it open?

Grandparent mentors, in working with young people to care for and preserve the environment, should remember to tell the story of creation either by reading it together from Genesis or telling it in their own words. In doing so, grandparents can help the child to discover that all creation comes from God as a gift. The grandparent guides the child in expressing how one should treat a gift: to receive it with gratitude by expressing "thanks"; to use it carefully and for the purpose for which it was intended; and always to share it with others.

Next, the grandparent explores how important creation was for Jesus while he lived on earth. This step could include identifying those stories and times in the Bible that illustrate how Jesus used nature as a basis for instruction or for religious signs and symbols. Vine and branches, water, fig trees, sparrows, and wheat are a few examples. Also, grandparents, together with their grandchildren, can explore passages from the Old Testament illustrating how nature speaks to us of God; for example, the canticle of the three youths cast into a fiery furnace, who called upon all nature to bless God (Dan 3:56-88).

A grandparent mentor and grandchild can read the story illustrating the Heavenly Father's awareness and care for the lilies of the field and the birds of the air and point out the lesson of God's personal love and care for them. For example, "Think of the lilies of the field; they never have to work or spin; yet I assure you that not even Solomon in all his regalia was robed like one of these. Now if that is how God clothes the grass in the field which is there today and thrown into the furnace tomorrow, will he not much more look after you?" (Mt 6:28-30).

At another time, grandparents can pick up on the religious theme underlying the value of creation by guiding the child in probing what would happen if we misuse or squander these precious gifts or selfishly acquire more for ourselves instead of sharing with those who have little? In concluding, together or separately, each can offer a spontaneous prayer—perhaps in gratitude for the gifts of creation.

Maybe grandparents, like actress Meryl Streep in responding to her son's question: "Do we own all this land and lakes where we live?" can remind grandchildren that "the earth is the Lord's and the fullness thereof" (Ps 23:1).

These examples show the approaches that modern grandparents can use in educating children to adopt environmentally needed values that will have an impact on our lives and those of future generations. Justice and gratitude call for preserving the planet and its resources for future generations. Enlightened grandparents realize that they have inherited the earth and have a responsibility to do all in their power to preserve it for those that live after them. What better way to do this than to transmit these values to the younger generation? Grandparent mentors have the time, knowledge, memory, and skills that can be used to accomplish this goal.

The Happy Apprentices

Frequently, I meet young or middle-aged adults who tell me about the influence their grandparents had in their lives. One of these women, Jackie, I met while enjoying the waves on the South Carolina Atlantic seacoast. Our discussion about children eventually led to reminiscences of her elderly grandmother, who had recently died in her nineties. She had lived with Jackie and her family in her later years. During her childhood, Jackie remembers her grandmother teaching her the secrets of making pastry. She took great pride in having perfected the poppyseed roll. She told Jackie it took years of trying various recipes and finally combining the best to get perfect results. Some of Jackie's treasured memories were those special moments as her grandmother gave her pointers on how to prepare the dough and poppyseed mixture and how to spread the mixture onto the dough. "Granny could probably do this in her sleep," she thought. When the rolls were taken from the oven, Granny would give Jackie the first piece to sample.

Jackie often teases her husband that Granny's poppyseed roll was the decisive factor prompting her husband to marry her. She recalled the first time her future husband-to-be came to their house for dinner. Jackie served a piece of the poppyseed roll that Granny had taught her to make. After tasting it, he exclaimed, "I would marry a woman who could make something like this!" One year later they were husband and wife.

Television's Hugh Downs learned from his early experiences with his grandmother how important it is to challenge youngsters as they move into adulthood. He credits his maternal grandmother with having had great expectations for him while he was growing up in Lima, Ohio. A bastion of Victorian morality, she had never doubted about what was right and wrong. She never talked down to her grandchildren, nor did she ever let them get away with anything. He remembers that as a boy he received books from his grandmother that were way over his head, such as the book by Osborn on anthropology. She just assumed that he would read them; and he did. His grandmother never babied him but demanded the same responsible behavior of him that she would of an adult. Such conduct was taken for granted.

The mentoring influence of Downs' grandmother now carries over to his own grandson, Sadim. When Sadim was in grade school, Downs bought him a horse. They have also traveled together to Scotland, Japan, Switzerland, Sweden, and Canada. In addition to going on wilderness trips together, they go sailing, soaring, and scuba diving. Downs admits that although these experiences have been fun, they are very challenging and a good way to prepare Sadim for adulthood.

When he and Sadim were in some tight spots, even dangerous ones, Sadim had to make the decisions without his grandfather's intervention. Down speaks with a mentor's pride as he admits that, like himself when he was young, Sadim rises to the occasion. This well-known television personality and proud grandfather is now making plans for crossing the Pacific in a sailboat together with his grandson.[7] One wonders what awaits Sadim's future grandson. How fortunate if Sadim carries on this tradition with his own children and grandchildren.

Peggy Flemming is another product of a grandparent's mentoring influence. Something of her grandfather has rubbed off on her. From him, she learned to be a real doer. Whatever he would do, he tried his hardest—whether it was playing ball with his grandchildren or walking three miles a day—until his death at eighty-nine.

Peggy's grandfather enjoyed doing things instead of hiring someone to do them for him. He would even buy do-it-yourself books and figure things out for himself. On big projects he would invite all his grandchildren to come and help.

One of her favorite memories is of her grandfather's gigantic garden at his home near San Francisco. Every morning she could go and pick out any fruit she wanted for her breakfast cereal—raspberries, boysenberries, or strawberries. Her grandfather worked very hard in the garden, and loved it.

Experiencing her grandfather as a hard worker has left its mark on Peggy. Like him, she always want to be out there participating. "I know I'll never want to be just a spectator," she says. Nineteen years after her Olympic triumph in Grenoble, France, Peggy continues to skate for special events and acts as a TV commentator.[8]

Program Opportunities

The role of mentoring is gaining popularity across the country. Many elders are participating in programs specifically geared toward mentoring. By becoming involved as mentors, grandparents are discovering new meaning in "giving" and in passing on their knowledge and skills to the younger generation, who often feel neglected due to the fragmentation within their immediate family. The larger society, too, benefits from grandparents who give back what someone once gave to them.

Growing numbers of grandparents are becoming mentors in a variety of ways. In Washington, D.C., the Senior Citizen/Latchkey Project provides an opportunity for grandparents to take part in recreational projects after school.

In Los Angeles, California, the Neighborhood Youth Association runs a program called Linking Lifetimes, one of eight nationwide programs that pair mentors who are fifty-five or older with adolescents. This program targets youth who need help and healthy older people who have been feeling unproductive. It provides elders with an opportunity to transmit some of their skills and experiences. This work enhances their own self-esteem and ties them into the rest of society. Eighty-three year old Fortino Diaz and his son Hector devote Sunday afternoons to fishing excursions or to playing baseball with twelve year old Jaime Gonzales and his thirteen year old brother Ben. Hector says that the boys are at an age where they can be influenced and, "We're hoping that we can steer them in the right direction." In talking about ordinary things like fishing, they also stress the importance of education and of striving for a better place in life. Their goal is to expose the boys to the better things in life as worth working for.

Similar teen-parenting programs operate in Ann Arbor, Michigan. Lifespan Resources matches older grandmothers with teen mothers in an effort to prevent child abuse. These grandmothers provide friendship, counseling, and training in life skills.

Retired union members and other grandparents within communities in Springfield, Massachusetts, are giving one-to-one support to young offenders in an alternative sentencing program. The youth receive help from grandparent mentors in finding and maintaining employment and in learning how to "navigate" the system.

An increasing number of schools are recognizing the value of getting grandparent mentors into the classroom. Schools vary in their approach. Some high schools have grandparents participating in democracy classes, in which they give presentations pertaining to history and social change. Other schools enlist the help of grandparent mentors as aides in classes such as reading, mathematics, and crafts.

In Pittsburgh, under a program developed by Generations Together at the University of Pittsburgh, retired seniors who have special talents—writers, musicians, sculptors, painters, artisans, and dancers—support the arts in the schools by serving as mentors. Everyone benefits. "When you're old, it is refreshing to be with the young," is the feeling of the grandparents involved. On the other hand, by working with a mentor, the young can gain a chance to see how a real artist works and what it is like to pursue a career. David Uranish expressed his delight as he remarked, "He just sets down a block of clay, and we go at it." At the end of the year an art display is assembled celebrating the fruits of this intergenerational effort. These mentors, although retired, have discovered new meaning in rechanneling their energies into the future, into today's youth.

On Mondays at the Annandale Health Care Day Center For Older Adults in Annandale, Virginia, an intergenerational program is underway. A small group of seniors walk to the other half of the facility to interact with children and engage in planned games and activities. On other days the children visit with the seniors and engage in special activities such as songs, exercises, games, and storytelling. These elderly mentors assist cognitively impaired children in gaining self-confidence as learners.

In Columbia, Maryland, one library has a Grandparent Place located in the Children's Department of the Central Library where grandparent volunteers are available daily to read to and interact with the younger library users. Several times a year library grandparents plan and present theme programs such as sharing "memory" tales and activities from their childhoods.

Another successful mentoring program called the Northumberland Program focuses on children who have difficulty being mainstreamed into regular schools. Children meet weekly with a resident of Frey Nursing Home in Middleburg, Pennsylvania. There young and old become friends and partners in various activities. One such project involved kite decorating. Working together provides young people an opportunity to discover aspects of their personality that never had a chance to be developed. Older people have an outlet for self-giving. Relating one-to-one fosters an atmosphere for the emergence of positive qualities through corroboration on special projects. As a result of this program, underprivileged children have healthier attitudes and behavior changes than they would in a regular school setting.

What makes these kinds of programs that link grandparent mentors to juvenile offenders so successful? One reason is that mentors do not give up; they are tenacious. They keep coming back even if kids don't always show up for an appointment. Youths who have often been disappointed by adults are prone to test other adults.

Mentors realize they are not going to change young people overnight. Helping them to achieve small successes will increase their self-esteem. By not giving up, having realistic expectations, and offering a real commitment, mentors can be especially meaningful to the young.

Learning centers for retirees are springing up around the country. Usually they are attached to a university or college. For example, the University of North Carolina, Ashville, sponsors the Center for Creative Retirement and draws teachers from various fields such as engineering and sociology. These retirees mentor young persons aspiring toward a career in a particular discipline.

The University of Maryland's Golden I.D. Program has about one-hundred-fifty elders involved in being mentors to others, in taking classes, and in assisting at the various levels of university management.

In Florida, the Academy of Senior Professionals, a learning in retirement center at Eckerd College, accommodates people who have distinguished themselves in a wide range of disciplines. Members can serve as "discussant colleagues"—experts who visit undergraduate classes and offer opposing views on a variety of topics. Some of these experts teach at community high schools as well. What is special about these programs is that the mentors add a perspective that only their generation can offer.

These examples show how grandparents are becoming involved as mentors around the country, not only to their own grandchildren, but also to others of the younger generation.

Mrs. Barbara Bush affords a good example. Tom Brokaw of NBC referred to her as "America's Surrogate Grandmother" because of her great involvement in education. Mrs. Bush visits schools and other places to teach children to love books. She does this by reading to children, who are naturally eager for stories. Besides her own twelve grandchildren, Mrs. Bush has found a place in her heart for other grandchildren.[9]

Eighty-eight year old Maggie Kuhn, the national convener of the social activist organization, the Gray Panthers, believes that younger and older generations must work together. The secret is in forging an alliance of interest between both groups. She offers this sound advice to the young:

> Find an old friend, an old person who can be your friend. And you and that old person can give each other a great deal of good advice. You can be teaching and learning from each other every step of the way, and both lives will be enriched and made more exciting and viable because you've been together.

Whenever and wherever the young and old discover each other, the elder generation—as wise counselors, guides, directors, teachers, and mentors—have an abundant opportunity to influence the future. For today's children are tomorrow's decision makers.

Tips on Teaching Skills

1. Develop a relationship with a young person—either your own grandchild or someone else. Be consistent and faithful in spending time with that person.
2. Foster a nurturing relationship. This is the foundation for successful mentoring.
3. Use special moments and new experiences as opportunities for mentoring, e.g., trips to the zoo, museum, circus, park, and church; current events: peace works, elections, scientific discoveries, sports, and environmental issues.
4. Tell stories to impart information and wisdom and to teach them about their moral and religious heritage. You may be the only one to do so.
5. Provide opportunities for a young person to be responsible and to accept the consequences for one's choices; choosing one thing means the elimination of other possibilities.
6. Vary your technique in teaching to keep interest and enthusiasm alive.
7. Stretch their potential by offering them challenges within their reach. Do not talk down to a young person. Respect where they are in their development.
8. Be on the lookout for their special gifts, talents, and interests. Foster these through praise and further exploration. Look for opportunities that will encourage their development.
9. Reserve time for sharing your own talents, hobbies, or skills. Capitalize on the ones the child enjoys doing.
10. Remember: A mentor's role takes various forms: observant bystander, fellow learner, involved teacher, and wise guide.

4

GRANDPARENTS AS *MODELS OF AGING:* FACING THE FUTURE

Louis Sullivan, former Secretary of Health and Human Services, in one of his addresses, quoted an expert on parenting as saying: "What you do deliberately doesn't matter as much as who you are, and kids have a way of finding out."

He went on to say that our children need to find out that there are adults who care enough to provide consistently genuine love, teach strong values, develop good character, and that there are adults who are models of real integrity.[1]

Dr. Sullivan's words include grandparents. But how can a grandparent make the connection between who he or she is and being a model of integrity? Having a sense of fate and destiny can help grandparents discover what they are and what they are called to be.

A grandmother can begin by reflecting on herself as having been dealt a particular hand in life. For example, she was born into a certain family, inherited certain traits, tendencies, strengths, and weaknesses, and given a fair amount of talent. That grandmother might have a certain number of grandchildren over which she has had no say. All of these facets make up some of the raw materials of life—the givens. They cannot be changed. That is what can be considered one's "fate" in life.

A grandparent, however, can play her hand whichever way she wants. She does not have to remain a passive observer allowing life's circumstances to dictate her attitudes and aspirations. She has the freedom to choose how she plans to shape her circumstances and attitudes—as an active participant in her own destiny. Grandparents, by the way they decide to live, do not have to be dominated by fate, but can choose to respond in such a way that others gain inspiration and hope. Grandparents who make an effort to follow their destiny are being true to themselves and to God, the giver of all gifts. Their lives tell the story of what can happen when someone makes wise and courageous decisions. They become models of integrity and, indeed, true models of aging.

Why a Model of Aging?

Life is a journey which begins at conception. Each life has its own peculiar destiny, yet somehow it intertwines with those of others. Finding ourselves to be immigrants in time, we experience the same life stages—infancy, childhood, adolescence, adulthood, old age and death—as others do, yet in different existential settings. Those who are years ahead of us in age have had different historical experiences yet share current ones with us as well. All of us, however, must ever relinquish old and familiar settings and move toward the unknown.

But we need not go alone and unprepared. Always we find those along the way who have already passed through our stage of life. From them we garner clues about life's themes or gain some sense of direction about how to be and what to do when faced with the challenges and blessings of life and love. We learn, too, how to avoid pitfalls and how to stand firm in adversity.

Today especially there is need to overcome a cultural perspective that looks at aging as a time of depletion and deprivation—a time of unavoidable catastrophe. No wonder the elderly and middle-aged alike think of aging with fear and growing panic. As time goes by they resort to extraordinary means to conceal the physical imprint of their true age. Even self-esteem is sacrificed on the altar of perpetual youth. It is the task of the elderly and the young to shatter these myths of a fading future. As models of aging, grandparents manifest the lasting values that counter the myths of ageism. They show their children and grandchildren that the best things about being human last a lifetime.

A danger for those who lead the way, however, is that they "think" they know what the younger ones are experiencing by inferring from their own past experiences. The result may be that the younger and older live in different realms of discourse. Unless both generations are willing to learn from each other, they are deprived of continuity and interconnectedness, and a common language.

We meet others who act as signposts through the journey of life first of all in the family. They provide the means for discovering our circumstanced uniqueness. Within the three-generational family we learn the patterns of behavior and skills that accompany each person's role. We discover what it means to be a father, a mother, a child, a brother, a sister, an aunt, an uncle, and a grandparent. The implications are long-range. For example, we are presently discovering the impact of child abuse on later adult parental behavior. People tend to repeat the cycle of abuse unless there is some measure of intervention. Fortunately, people also repeat cycles of love and support.

The various roles within the family continue from one generation to another, although the persons fulfilling these roles change. Beginning as a daughter she becomes a sister, wife, aunt, mother, mother-in-law, and grandmother. An aunt or uncle interacting with their niece or nephew transmits characteristics and patterns of behavior that in turn become identified with that role. The characteristics of that role are then transmitted to succeeding generations who then take over. There is always someone with needs to be met by someone who plays a particular role. A mutual "give and take" experience exists in role relationships. But always, as one's life moves on through different stages, new roles await.

Roles are patterns of behavior that usually are learned from other family members. The American version of a tale by the Brothers Grimms told anew by Brian Haggerty in *Out of the House of Slavery* (p. 82), gives us cause to reflect on the impact of our actions stemming from our role in the family.

> Grandmother no longer has full control over her muscles. Her hands tremble, and from time to time she breaks a dish while eating. Frustrated, her daughter gives her a wooden bowl and tells her from now on she must eat out of it. When granddaughter asks why grandmother no longer eats from china plates like the rest of the family, mother replies, "Because she is old." After a moment the child tells her mother, "You must save the wooden bowl when grandmother dies." "Why?" asks the woman. The child answers, "For when you are old." Quickly grandmother's wooden bowl is replaced with a china one and she is again treated as the other members of the family.[2]

Because of their special place in the generational family, grandparents can be a major influence on the younger generation by claiming their rightful role as grandparents—people who are ahead of other generations on the journey of life. Erik Erikson calls this last stage of life the "grand-generative" aspect of old age. This general grandparenthood should play a useful and reciprocal role in the life of children. Both the old and young can benefit from the energizing effects at this stage.

Some grandparents, unfortunately, have allowed cultural opinions, such as age-segregated living, to sway them in the direction of non-involvement (different from non-interference) and, as a result, deprive the family of needed support, with its emotional bonding. Likewise, parents who cut their children off from grandparents deprive them of an important level of interaction.

Grandparents, however, can be a connecting link between the past and the present and serve to interpret through their actions and attitudes what is valuable and meaningful to the family and community. If grandparents choose to adopt the values of modern society, if they have a greater concern for themselves than for their children and grandchildren's future, or if they give priority to their own desires over the needs of others, then they put in jeopardy the traditional collective values that have stabilized society. Foremost among these values is a sense of obligation and sacrifice that have characterized the sound family life upon which a healthy society depends. Grandparents have learned first-hand how to translate those values into practical everyday living. Those same values need to be passed on to the next generation, if the family is to remain the seat of caring and support in a fast changing society.

The Power of Example

As models of aging grandparents can influence the future through their grandchildren. In doing so, they will help to resolve the current conflict of interest that many experience, manifested in the tension between personal autonomy and family bonding.

"What does it mean to be a model of aging?" asked one grandmother. Aging is not a series of established time slots. Too often we tend to think of aging in linear patterns. We begin at one point and end up at another. Of course, some grandparents are very old; others are fairly young. But even in the same age group, many find themselves in very different roles: some are parents, others are grandparents, and still others are divorced or widowed, healthy or sick. Furthermore, chronological and biological age diverge amazingly.

Nevertheless, when we speak of aging we implicitly relate it to the various changes that all eventually undergo. A strong emphasis, however, has been placed on the physical losses that accompany the aging process. That is not to say, however, that there are not mental, emotional, and spiritual changes that we experience as we mature. Aging, then, implies passing through the various levels and stages of our development from infancy through maturity to senescence. Our environment, our experiences, and our responses, help to shape what we become at every age.

As a grandparent one has already tasted and tested life through a segment of time in the flow of history. A person has thus acquired certain strengths, skills, awareness, attitudes, and values that give shape and form to their lives. Of course, fears and failures are present, too, in this less than perfect world. But for the most part, as they grow old people learn to appreciate and foster values and virtues, which they want for their children and grandchildren. Grandparents acquire these habits, good or bad, not only in crises and calamities, but also in everyday living. This ongoing development is what they have to offer as they relate to members of the younger generation.

A graphic description of a model of aging in the eyes of a grandchild was illustrated in a letter sent to Louise Kern, from her sixteen year old granddaughter, Rachel. Louise shared this letter with me in hopes that other grandparents might be influenced by its message. After all, the best feedback on the potential of grandparents as models of aging is from the younger generation themselves. This following letter resulted from a school assignment and was to be written to the one most admired and loved by the student. It was done at a time of heightened concern over the possibility of a nuclear holocaust during the Cold War.

Dear Nana,

I know you won't survive this anymore than I will. I just want to say you've been the most wonderful grandmother a person can have. I hope you die quickly and without pain, and I hope there is life after death so that I could see you there.

Like I said, you've been a really nice grandmother, a good friend—someone who has sympathized with me when I had problems, praised my efforts, treated me with respect.

I'll always remember (as long as I'm able) the way

we came over on Sundays. Your food was always good—"Just an experiment" you'd say—but your experiments always turn out good. You are such a selfless person, Nana. If you were reading this now you would just laugh and say that it is a pleasure to do what you can for people. And that's true.

You always put others first and yourself last, but not like a martyr or something—just because it's natural with you. You never think about those things. You just do it.

You always find it so easy to love people, Nana. I don't know how but you do. You'd talk to a kid with a Mohawk haircut at the bus stop, and ask him about his life and really care. And that squirrel that has been coming to your window for the nuts you give it— you care about that squirrel.

Whenever you call us on the phone and I answer, you talk to me and ask how things are, and you laugh at the funny things. You're not the kind of person that you don't want to tell certain things to. You don't judge, you just listen. Mostly, you love—and I love you.

Rachel

Louise first told me about this letter when I met her at a senior center in Maryland. At that time she hesitated about mentioning the letter to the other grandparents. Her impression was that they might think she was bragging. She had been told that some of the characteristics of one's personality live on for generations. From the look on her face I could tell she was pleased with this thought. Perhaps it was because she saw part of herself and the good life she stood for living on in her granddaughter.

Why should grandparents hesitate about sharing the accolades paid by their grandchild? Is it because society has not encouraged a role for them, such as being a model of aging? That is, after all, what should be expected of grandparents. If they realized this, grandparents might make a greater effort to share more deeply in the lives of the young who stand ready to accept models. Think of all the media stars or sports figures that become idols for the young. Their influence often fills a void in young lives. Yet those who are truly nearest to them in the natural arrangement of a family have a first-hand opportunity to communicate what life is really about in its full context of human relationships.

Grandparents who are aging gracefully have already begun to make a difference. Louise Kern's letter from her granddaughter gives voice to this fact. In Rachel's eyes, Louise is an exemplar of a truly beautiful person possessing virtues that underlie our secret strivings for excellence. Perhaps what happens when our minds and hearts are moved by a "model of aging," is that the truth we carry within our hearts somehow resonates when it recognizes that truth outside of itself. The result is a harmony of spirit that brings its own energy in moving us to strive toward the same.

Forty-three year old Sonia sat quietly in the hospital room where her eighty-two year old father lay. For several moments she was absorbed by the many thoughts running through her mind taking her back in time. She remembered how her father was when she was a child. The contrast between the past and the present was striking. Now he lay dying of heart failure, dependent on others to anticipate his every need, for he had difficulty in communicating. She was fortunate, however, to have experienced his strong fatherly love despite his sufferings. With great effort he lifted his body slightly, opened his eyes, and managed a broad smile in her direction when he first became aware of her presence. Then he slumped back and that painful look reappeared, accentuated by the oxygen tube in his nose.

As his daughter, Sonia felt the bond of love renewed—that close attachment formed throughout the years between her father and herself. Somehow through that simple smile her father reassured her of the biblical truth that love is strong as death. She would always hold that memory close to her heart.

Sonia remembered when her father and mother became

grandparents. How proud they were of their grandchildren. By now there were two—both teenagers—and the grandfather never tired of being brought up to date about their lives and experiences. They realized that, too, and kept in close touch. For example, his eighteen year old granddaughter drove over two hundred miles with her girl friend to visit her grandfather when she learned he had an attack of shingles. Delighted by this, her grandfather would often refer to her as his "pal."

As Sonia thought about her father's positive attitude in living, she realized that his approach toward death was no different than toward life. He was a man of hope with a smiling heart. Sitting there, she could not help but admire her aged father who gave her courage to face her own uncertain days ahead.

When we consider grandparents as models of aging, we view them from the perspective not only of what they have done, such as surviving the vicissitudes of life while contributing as best they could to the family and community, but also of what they have manifested spiritually in responding to the realities of daily living. After all, our vocation in life involves both being and becoming. These touch our innermost core where Christ dwells in our hearts through love. Grandparents have a special call to love, which requires fully losing themselves. It is in losing ourselves that we find ourselves, and in the process we put on Christ—the way, the truth, and the light.

In the Jewish tradition, grandparents draw life from the Torah (scripture, revelation, law, story) which is for them the way, the truth, and the light pointing toward God. Drawing upon the written Torah, grandparents become for grandchildren the walking Torah—teaching youngsters how to walk before their God while being faithful to family, tradition, and ritual.

On one hand, Christian grandparents find religious meaning in the death and resurrection themes of scripture. On the other hand, Jewish grandparents relate to the religious meaning found in the themes of sorrow and joy, as symbolized by bittersweet food at the Seder meal.

All grandparents who love, however, convey a strong sense of presence that goes out to others. Action devoid of a loving presence is limp or rigid. Grandparents, motivated by love, are that loving presence that makes all the difference when flexibly relating to others. "Just by being there," one grandchild proclaimed, "my grandmother seems to make tough moments easier to bear."

A grandparent who is truly present to a grandchild becomes a model of respect and care. Knowing that in relating in a loving and kindly manner, they are like the heartbeat of God. A sense of his goodness becomes real. What they do takes on a deeper dimension—a stronghold in the memory of a grandchild.

Although grandparents may find themselves in changing circumstances, they always have the capacity to love and to be loved. One may, for example, find himself no longer able to carry out the daily functions and demands of life. A sick bed may be one's call to be a "sabbath" grandparent—one who, like God, rested after the work was done. But the love in their heart can still be directed toward those who come into their presence as Sonia's father had done.

But what about those grandparents who have been afflicted with debilitating diseases? In such cases grandparents become models of the mysteries of God who is calling those dear to them to place a tremendous hope in his loving providence who, in the end, makes all things new.

Passing Years

Modern grandparents are living libraries, the repositories whose lives bear witness that it is possible to adjust to enormous change—and, indeed, to thrive. Those who lived before World War II know this better than those who came after. As Margaret Mead says, they know that something can be done because they were alive during the Depression and did something about it.[3]

Grandparents shine as models of adaptability. From them

we learn to have faith in the future. Fear of the future can cause us to cling desperately to the security of the present. Many young people today find themselves caught up in the anguish of separation, divorce or death of parents. Most experience peer pressure and the demands of everyday life. In addition, economic recession, pollution, burgeoning crimes, possible wars, and planetary devastation loom over them. More than ever before, the active presence of long-lived people can be deeply reassuring symbols of survival.

As models of aging, grandparents possess a broader and more confident perspective about life and its meaning and value. This perspective envisages a place for death. Such widened horizons require maturity and poise that does not come automatically. Maturity—exercising one's potential reasonably and responsibly—results from personal attitudes and commitments in an ongoing response to life. Graceful living inspired by a faith fruitful in good works; grateful recognition that one lives through the goodness of God; sensitivity to the needs of other people, active responsiveness to those needs; self-discipline, especially of the tongue; freedom from the tyranny of desire; realistic acceptance of human limitations; and steadfastness and hope grounded in love—all contribute to a meaningful life. "Since the Spirit is our life, let us be directed by the Spirit" (Gal 5:25). What one is, is expressed in the outward patterns of life.

Many grandparents through realizing the meaning of life can prepare peacefully for death. In large part, this comes from assurances such as St. Paul's that there is a fuller life awaiting after death. These positive expectations extend to physical creation which is also to be redeemed and renewed in a way paralleling the redemption of human beings (see Rom 8:18-25). Grandparents, by word and example, have the potential to communicate those spiritual values to the younger generation. Seeing them exemplified in the elders, young people can more readily find meaning and value in the present, and at the same time find encouragement and hope for the future.

Not that the elderly have a monopoly on the process of

integrating the past, the present, and the future, but as seasoned pilgrims they have been to places in the psyche not yet visited by the young. They know and understand the territory of life and should stand ready to guide others along the paths ahead. Long-lived people bring something of the past with which to inform the present. These memories, transcending the immediate present, provide for the future. Grandparents, after many years of meeting life's challenges and struggles, have earned the privilege of a special role assessing new challenges. They can rightfully exercise their privilege to help young people keep their faith in human destiny and the divine presence.

Keeping Flexible

In investigating the lives of active though relatively "ancient" grandparents, we look for clues as to what has made their lives worthwhile. John Kirk, from his interviews with more than 200 centenarians, is convinced that it is virtually impossible to have reached one's 100th birthday without having made a mark on the community.[4] Whether involved in local or national affairs, they all have influenced America's destiny and their spirit remains positive about having lived so long.

One centenarian, Jay Hoover, said he could not think of a more interesting, action-packed or thrilling 100 years. Jay can recount times from covered wagon days to the lunar landing module, from a time of isolated communities to one of instant global communications. Overcoming obstacles is what Jay understands firsthand. This is true when it comes to the difficulties imposed by living in isolation. Piney Lakes country south of Burns, Oregon, a sparsely populated area even now, was where Jay was born. There was a severe winter freeze at the time, and the only way to fetch a midwife was by using ice skates. "My father skated all the way to the midwife's ranch. Then the two of them skated back," Hoover recalled.

These exceptional great, and even great-great grandparents, can show the younger generation how to get the most out of life or, on the other hand, how to make the most of life. The best preparation for old age is to begin early to open oneself to the truths, values, and commitments which make life worthwhile.

From studies of this age group certain characteristics seem to prevail. For the most part they have tended to be physically active people and exude a love of life. Although Iva Blake now uses a wheelchair, she still manages to cultivate one of the best backyard gardens in Albuquerque. There's no stopping her from taking up the hoe and the rake and doing the weeding and watering, beginning in early spring through late autumn. She even has specially designed cut-off tools to assist her, Kirk notes.

Another centenarian grandparent exemplifies a trait typical of many in this age group: self-discipline, the setting of standards. Julius Adler dresses himself immaculately each day in a shirt, pants, and tie and has a suit jacket handy for when company comes. He's made it a practice never to be caught in shorts or a bathrobe. He follows this rule rigorously.

Grandparents in this special age group tend to be people-centered. They seek to help the less fortunate. Ella Miller's philosophy—"God intended us to reach out to others"—is in line with her actions. Until moving to Virginia, she worked one day a week at a volunteer food and clothing bank for the poor at a local church in Cincinnati. As president of a women's philanthropic club, she frequently visited less-robust elderly people in nursing homes. One creative grandparent expressed it thus: "In giving of self, you become energized."

Unlike a significant segment of the teen generation today who have little faith in the future, the centenarian grandparents continue to make plans and to look forward to the years ahead. One man hoped to treat himself to an Alaskan cruise for his hundredth birthday. Upon discovering that all the cabins had been taken until May, he requested to be booked for the following year.

When Marjorie Stonewall Douglas was being interviewed on her hundredth birthday by NBC nightly news, she said: "I can't hear and can't see, but I'm healthy." She is now writing a book, which she dictates to a secretary. Marjorie, a conservationist, is credited with helping to save the Everglades, and she was instrumental in it's being named a national park.

John Kirk also discovered that most centenarians enjoy active spiritual lives. They have hope in a higher power outside of themselves. They acknowledge that there is a divine being that is greater than they. This sensitivity to the transcendent attunes them to a larger purpose and gives direction to their lives. Many who have walked in faith have found peace in later life and do not fear death.

Rose Kennedy, over a hundred, remains a model of strength for her children and grandchildren. She keeps alive the faith in public service that was begun by her own father (three-term congressman and two-term mayor of Boston). She has long been a model for the nation. Congress cited Mrs. Kennedy's "commitment to the central role of the family in American life and proclaimed her birthday as a day for the nation to appreciate families with appropriate ceremonies and activities."

Rose's faith and strong commitment to family is a driving force and source of meaning in her life, notes journalist Coleman McCarthy. She believes that a family was best kept together by fidelity to religion. Her family-oriented faith was rooted in her childhood: "Every night during Lent, my mother would gather us in one of the rooms of the house, turn out the lights—the better to concentrate—and lead us in reciting the rosary. I'm sure my knees ached and that sometimes I wondered why I should be doing all the kneeling and studying and contemplating and praying. And I became understanding and grateful."

Throughout her life Mrs. Kennedy's attention to God was reflected in her attention to family, especially when difficulties and sorrow came along. Like her mother, she persevered in daily mass and in the daily recitation of the rosary.

Going back to biblical times, we find another elder, Simeon, whose life was attentive to the spirit of God. He stands as a model of faith, hope, and piety—a man dedicated to God.

Awaiting for a whole lifetime for the coming of the messiah, he was richly rewarded in being able to actually hold the child Jesus in his arms. He rejoiced: "Lord, now you can let your servant go in peace, just as you promised; because my eyes have seen the salvation which you have prepared for all the nations to see" (Lk: 29-31). Simeon's contemporary, Anna the prophetess, was at least eighty-four years old and yet active and alert as she kept vigil in the temple. A woman of prayer, she celebrated the coming of Jesus as the redemption of Jerusalem and held her savior in her arms (Lk 2:37-38).

Armed with resiliency of spirit and moral strength, these elders discovered for themselves the value of living a long life, when it is lived well.

Physically Fit

Swimming, running, and weight lifting are not just for high school and college students or for professional athletes and olympians. Today's misnamed "over the hill" grandparents, those past fifty, are picking up speed. Realizing that a healthy and long life depends on more than controlling disease, a new breed of grandparents find themselves doing whatever it takes to be physically fit—and are enjoying it! Some have formed groups such as the 70+ Ski Club that has members in their seventies, eighties, and nineties. Others, such as retired real estate investor Eric de Reynier, of Albany, California, took up hang gliding when he was seventy-two and was still at it in his eighties. Then there is Hilda Crooks of Loma Linda, California, who climbed Mt. Whitney for the twenty-third time—at age ninety.

It is no secret that Barbara Bush and Texas Governor Ann Richards, both grandmothers, routinely exercise. For Mrs. Bush it's swimming; for Governor Richards it's walking three miles twice a week. Other grandmothers find time for aerobic dancing. Eula Weaver, at age eighty-two, suffered from angina, congestive heart failure, high blood pressure, and arthritis. In five years, she won ten gold medals for running in the National Senior Olympics. Her secret—a proper diet and exercise.

Sports contribute abundant models of aging. For example, in the twentieth running of the New York Marathon in 1989, about twelve percent entered were fifty years of age or older, and more than 400 were sixty or older. In fact, three men were over ninety. They had run their first marathons at the ages of seventy-three, seventy-six, and seventy-seven. That year for the first time there was a ninety-year-old in the race. The oldest woman to participate was eighty-one. That same year, a 4 foot 10 1/2 inch, 100 pound woman ran in the Boston Marathon. She was eighty-eight years old and had run her first marathon at seventy-two.

These models of aging rebut the false assumptions about life after fifty. They offer a vision, not only to their peers, but also to the younger generation, of what can be accomplished by stretching one's potential during the second half of life. The message is clear: people can enjoy good health and vigor even at an advanced age.

For others, despite health problems, life can still be productive and happy. Take, for example, French artist Auguste Renoir. At sixty, his fingers were so stiff, he could not hold a brush, and he was unable to walk. Yet he continued to paint for eighteen more years—working with a brush strapped to his wrist.

Besides dispelling myths about health and aging, grandparents of all ages are taking issue with myths about sexuality. Among the growing number of voices, including Maggie Kuhn's, founder of the Grey Panthers, affirming that sexuality is alive and well after sixty is octogenarian and journalist Chalmers Roberts. Roberts, a grandfather of seven, acknowledges that sex at eighty may not be what it was at thirty, but it still has a special delight, though with—"a different sense of timing... a different mode of agony and ecstasy."[5] For him, sensual sexuality is less a matter of age than it is of maturity. Mutual sexuality is the kind that continues and even improves with age.[6] Chalmers noted, that according to the Talmud, at the age of eighty, men and women acquire the power of *gevurah*—the new strength of advanced age. Here is someone, a little older than Chalmers, who illustrates this point.

The words, "I want to die young at an advanced age," characterized the life of another octogenarian, the educator, journalist, and scholar of American history—Max Lerner. Admittedly, he had lived a stormy and tempestuous life until his death in 1992 at the age of eighty-nine. Despite a series of illnesses—ranging from lymphoma in 1980 (he was given six months to live), to prostate cancer (contained by hormones), to a heart attack in 1984—he was absorbed with new possibilities for living. "I am neither an optimist nor a pessimist, but a possibilist," he once wrote. His legacy for his nine grandchildren and three great-grandchildren includes his lifelong celebration of sexuality, as his book, *Eros in America*, confirms.[7] To the end he was writing, lecturing, and teaching on diverse subjects. These public figures reassure us all by their amazing display of human vitality.

The Fruits of Maturity

In 1986, officer Steven McDonald was paralyzed for life by a bullet. From this came unspeakable grief—and a deeper vision.[8] It all began when he stopped one of three men in Central Park for questioning, was shot three times and, as a result, became a quadriplegic. He depends on his wife, Patti Ann, and others around him for everything he needs.

The assailant, a juvenile defendant, was sentenced to up to ten years in prison but was paroled after six. Asked his opinion of the sentence, Steven says, "I never really thought about it. We just wanted to put all our energies into a better future." He did so very successfully. Steven has been named National Father of the Year, and chosen Man of the Year by a dozen organizations. He is in constant demand for appearances at events such as the New York State Games for the Physically Challenged, Notre Dame football games, hospital functions, and charity fund-raisers. He has appeared on TV talk shows. At the baptism of his son, he received congratulations from the Governor of New

York, the Cardinal Archbishop of New York, and the President of the United States.

Steven's wounds were so severe they expected him to die, but he did not. One thing that kept him from death was his own spirit. The support of his wife, friends, other officers, and clergy, including Cardinal John J. O'Connor, helped to sustain him. After weaning himself from the painkilling drugs he had grown addicted to, he faced the challenge of the rest of his life. Dependent on a ventilator, he had to learn to speak again and to use a wheelchair by blowing into a tube.

Why did he become a police officer in the first place? Like his father and grandfather, he wanted to help people. With his indomitable spirit he still finds a way to get outside himself in spite of his grief and pain. He has a remarkable effect on others.

The rest of the story is significant. Fifty years ago, before the McDonald shooting, a New York City police officer was severely wounded while trying to stop a holdup in the Bronx. In spite of his wound, he got into the car and in the pursuing gun battle shot the tires out on the bandits' car. Then he collapsed. Although the officer never fully recovered, he returned to active duty and continued to help people. That officer was James J. Conway, Steven McDonald's grandfather. People may wonder why, after having been injured so severely himself, Steven McDonald would return to the police force to help others. James J. Conway would have understood.

As aging persons—and that includes everyone—we are all called to maturity. Maturity refers to a condition or quality of existence, not of age. Aging should foster maturity. Maturity, however, is not something automatic. It comes as a growth experience through sound decision making, and cuts across chronological age. It is adult to be mature as it is infantile to be immature. To be spiritually mature is to be not vulnerable to "every wind of doctrine" so that, being grounded in truth "we may grow up in all things in toward him who is the head, Christ" (Eph 4:14-15).

When Jesus took the little children in his arms, blessed

them and said, "I tell you solemnly, anyone who does not welcome the kingdom of God like a child will never enter it" (Mk 10:15), he was pointing to the positive qualities that accompany growth. How can this message be related to grandparents and their call to maturity? As paradoxical as this passage may sound, Jesus points to the childlike qualities required to enter the kingdom, i.e., to be trustful, to be open, to be teachable. Otherwise there is the danger, not only for the elderly but also for the young, of becoming rigidly fixed in one's ways. Early in life, some people already exhibit closed minds. Others, like Einstein, remained open even late in life to creative energy and new possibilities. Erik Erikson referred to Einstein as the "victorious child who never lost his sense of wonder."

The opposite of being "childlike" is being "childish" like children displeased with whatever is offered them or not wanting to face the truth about something for fear of repercussions. As a person matures there should be, according to Erikson's psychosocial scale of development, a growth in love, care, and wisdom. The words of Micah, the last of the four great eighth century Jewish prophets, bear repeating as a reminder. The way of fulfilment requires of us: "To do justice, and to love kindness, and to walk humbly with your God" (Mic 6:8).

Love for Learning

Regenerative grandparents do not exemplify the old proverb, "You can't teach an old dog new tricks." Although they may be physically impaired, they take the lead as teachers and as learners.

My uncle Joe lived like that until his death at eighty-two. When he retired at sixty-five, he challenged himself by learning to paint. He soon surprised many in our family with gifts of oil paintings. One painting portrays an early historical scene of the area where he lived. When he died the local newspaper featured him in a lengthy article and told how he attracted the children of the neighborhood. This five-foot-ten grandparent was loved by the neighborhood children who were eager to spend time with him, to watch him paint. Many had their parents buy them paints and got uncle Joe to get them started. At least two went on to a career in art.

Modern day models of aging are resuming their studies, sometimes for a university degree, sometimes just for the fun of it. Many are taking advantage of Elderhostel programs offered at some 1,500 colleges and universities in the United States and abroad. These grandparents communicate the message that learning is a lifelong need. The more they do so, the greater the chance that this principle becomes normative for society.

While kids moan about their homework, grandparents can exemplify the joys of learning. Schooling is not just for youngsters; it is an adventure for all ages. This move by the elderly can help to shape a new way of thinking that will enrich life and enhance its meaning. Love for learning has far-reaching effects. It can counteract the existential malaise that infects the lives not only of many young people, but also of many elders who, after retirement, find themselves, as someone facetiously remarked, "to be wondering in the desert."

The late Rabbi Abraham Joshua Heschel, a most respected Jewish voice to Catholics and Protestants, criticized some of the programs designed for those in retirement, as programs devised to help the aged become children.

> Now preoccupation with games and hobbies, the over-emphasis on recreation, while certainly conducive to eliminating boredom temporarily, hardly contributes to inner strength. The effect is rather, a pickled existence, preserved in brine with spice.... The goal, is not to keep the old man busy, but to remind him, that every moment is an opportunity for greatness. Inner purification is at least as important as hobbies and recreation.[9]

Eric Hoffer notes that when people are bored, it's primarily with themselves. The consciousness of a barren, meaningless existence is the main fountainhead of boredom. According to Hoffer, those who seek mere pleasure and dissipation will never be satisfied.[10] This state of mind may also diminish the lives of some grandparents who have chosen not to be involved with the young, although they are not without abilities and opportunities to give to others the fruits of their hard-earned maturity. Heschel's words are a challenge to them to expand their perspective on life: "Living is not a private affair of the individual. Living is what man does with God's time, what one does with God's world."[11]

To Share a Vision

Enlightened grandparents readily make changes in their own lives that will have a positive influence on their grandchildren. Envisaging how they themselves wish to be and modeling themselves after the lives of God-attentive elders in the spirit of the Bible, will enable them to be ambassadors of the good news for the younger generation. The presence of regenerative grandparents involved in their own transformation process lends authenticity to the message they wish to send their grandchildren: "To be the best you can be." Striving toward this goal requires openness toward change and a constancy of resolve.

Reflecting on the many years they have lived through, enlightened grandparents realize that right living is an art as difficult as it is necessary. Most of us eventually discover that our basic mission in life is to love and to be what God has called us to be, even in the face of great odds. To live up to God's call touches upon a spiritual, intellectual, emotional, and physical transformation of the self. Grandparents can be the perfect witnesses to such an achievement.

Being the best we can with what we have is an expression of gratitude for what has been given us. And it can be a form of prayer. As grandparents cooperate in their regenerative process they can, in effect, be offering a prayer of gratitude. At the same time, regenerative grandparents can allow for God's creativity to continue to be made manifest in them and through them to others. Transformed grandparents who respond to the call to magnify the Lord become symbols of the incarnation and epiphany: God's becoming flesh and revealing his presence to all.

Regenerative grandparenting involves conscious choice. These choices effectively foster all aspects of their lives. Their own striving sows the seeds that become implanted in the minds and hearts of their grandchildren. Later in life, these seeds bear fruit. The younger generation thus moves ahead with empathy and compassion, toward becoming individuals of strength and justice. They also become models of love by exchanging a self-centered life for a selfless life.

Some grandparents, however, have doubts about whether or not their lives are worthwhile. In our society, there is an ambiguity about values and even a loss of values. As models of aging, grandparents' lives may run counter to the secularism of today's society. Unfortunately, many adults have sacrificed their values to win the approval of the younger generation, who in turn flaunt preferences that are in opposition to what the grandparent upholds as true and important.

Pauline, who lives in a retirement home, shared her deep concerns with other grandparents during a regenerative workshop session. She explained how she has always offered grace before meals in her home. When her two teenage grandchildren came to visit, she noticed that they were uncomfortable with her offering a prayer before a meal. She was uncertain how to respond to that kind of situation.

The participating grandparents decided: yes, her life should stand for certain values. By continuing to express these values freely she was sending her grandchildren a message about what was important to her as well as about the need of the human spirit to give thanks to the creator for the gifts of creation. She should think of herself as planting seeds that would later bear fruit in their lives, perhaps only after she dies. This clarification gave Pauline the meaning and peace she had longed for.

Sometimes people suddenly wake up wondering: What is

life all about? What have I done to make this a better world? What legacy have I left for those coming after me? Have I tried to be the best that I can be in spite of adversities? To avoid walking blindly through life, grandparents should take time to reflect on a vision or image of their hopes and dreams. Ideally this should be done early in life. But beginning where one finds oneself carries this message: that one's capabilities make a difference.

Mr. Sweeny, a very slender and frail looking eighty-nine year old man with a hearing impairment, shared a room with my father in a nursing home. He spent much of his time resting, but he managed to play a quiet role in our family conversations. Why was this so? Because Mr. Sweeny, during his waking intervals, always managed a positive attitude toward all who came in contact with him. He made an effort to smile and greet all pleasantly. Whenever he had a need, instead of making a demanding call, he might simply phrase his needs with a question, "Don't you think it would be better if I had some more light while I read the paper?" Long after my visits to the nursing home, Mr. Sweeny's spirit has lived on in my memory and makes me sensitive about my response to others. Mr. Sweeny has made a choice between being soured by the crosses of old age or creatively responding to his present life circumstances.

From a different point of view we can learn how not to act from those who have lived their many years without experiencing the fruits of personal transformation. Emily, widowed and living alone at the age of eighty, had telephone contact with only one of her three daughters. The other two did not bother to keep in touch with her.

I first met Emily as a social service worker when I was identifying the elderly in a local community. As she answered the door, I noticed her tall, delicate frame and unkempt appearance. She greeted me with a look of suspicion. Engaging her in conversation, I was startled to discover a sad commentary on life. Her speech, riddled with complaints about her adult children, proved just how embittered she had grown over the years. Beneath it all, however, I found a lonely person who had lost contact with the essentials of life. She was now reaping what she had sown earlier. The taste was a bitter taste, not only to her but to me as well.

As time went on, I found myself dreading to pay her a visit because, after departing, for quite awhile I would be saddened. Nonetheless, I felt sorry for Emily, who had reached the twilight years of life burdened with so much discontent and disgruntledness. This sour state was not what I intended for my future. But, in the meantime, what could I possibly do to help her?

Knowing that Emily was unable to care properly for her lawn, which had accumulated thousands of leaves during the fall, I asked one of my teenage volunteers to rake it. Later that day, I received a telephone call from Emily expressing her astonishment about the clean-up in her yard. Upon returning from the doctor, she discovered five bags of leaves clustered near the side of her house. "You must have had something to do with this," she concluded. For the first time I detected a cheerful tone in her voice. From that point, her attitude began to slowly change. She began to relate to Benny, the thirteen year old boy who periodically checked on her needs. By freely reaching out to this elder, Benny helped her to realize the goodness and kindness of others, and in so doing, he touched her human spirit. What began as a good deed by an eighth grader turned out to be an opportunity for an alienated grandmother to begin thinking about her relationship to others. Charity goes a long way.

Prior to our contact with Emily, her life was subject to happenstance. Without a sense of self-importance, Emily had no feeling of responsibility to others. What good was she? Anyway, who cared? Clearly her life was devoid of any identifiable aim as to how she wanted to direct her energies. Grandparents can ward off such an impoverished state of existence by claiming a worthwhile vision that is open to others. Every vision should include the type of lived statement one wishes one's life to make. What values do I want to communicate to the younger generations by my beliefs, attitude, and actions? What difference do I want to make in my grandchild's life? In my childrens' lives? In my community, locally and globally? What can I do to help preserve the planet and insure its well-being for future generations? What kind of example do I want to be to others? How do I wish to be remembered?

Sometimes just asking the right question can put us on track. Am I going through life and still keeping the gifts of the spirit alive—charity, joy, peace, patience, goodness, kindness, long-suffering, and fear of the Lord? It is encouraging to recall the words from scripture: "The virtuous will flourish in the courts of our God, still bearing fruit in old age, still remaining fresh and green, to proclaim that Yahweh is righteous" (Ps 92:13-15).

Green Grandparents

As models of aging, grandparents can send an important message about their environmental values. Relating properly to the world and all that is in it as a special gift from God, grandparents instill a kindly and respectful attitude toward creation.

Charles Fenyvesi pays tribute to his grandfather, who serves as a beacon in his life. In his book, *When the World Was Whole*, Fenyvesi describes his maternal grandfather, Karl Schwartz, as a master gardener and model farmer. His grandfather, who lived in a tiny village in northeastern Hungary, "managed several thousand acres of land—some inherited, some acquired, and some rented from aristocrats far wealthier than he." His life was tied to the rhythms of nature and coupled with a respect and care for creation. For modern day ecologists, Karl is in every sense a model.

A man of deep faith, Karl—who loved wheat fields and trees, roses and horses and rivers—would always remember to give thanks to God for the abundance of life. "In the spring, he would decorate his best open carriage and his two best horses with long, brightly colored ribbons, and take his wife and their children for a ride around all the lands he owned and leased to inspect the fresh green stalks of wheat." Then, as part of his annual ritual, he would cry out, "This is a good life," hug and kiss his wife and then chant a prayer of thanksgiving.[12] Summer would see another ceremonial tour. In August he would hire twenty-four men and twenty-four women to harvest the wheat while a chant was sung. When work was done the village crier would announce that the fields were open to all who wanted to pick the fallen wheat from the ground. His grandfather kept to the rule of the Bible—the poor were entitled to those gleanings along with the unharvested wheat left at the edges.

Karl often praised the locust trees for "having a bird singing on it one day and giving warmth as firewood the following day"—from a common saying in his village. He appreciated the horse chestnut trees in particular for their shady allées (a forest tamed yet still a forest) which were designed for contemplation as well as to shelter romance.

As for roses—Karl had selected ones of various hues and scents for his front yard. His admiration for them in their natural setting was so great, he did not permit them to be cut for vases. He would allow the fallen petals, however, "to be collected in wicker baskets and brought into the house to be kept for fragrance until they all dried up and turned brown."[13]

On his estate one observed the principles of conservation, preservation, and regeneration. With an abundance of potatoes, which grew into large tubers in the sandy soil, a whole production cycle ensued. They were turned into alcohol, and what was left over after the distillation process was used to feed cattle, which grew and fattened quickly. The cattle, in turn, produced good manure which was spread on all his fields every winter. A larger crop of potatoes along with wheat and tobacco resulted from the enriched soil.

Karl walked the earth in praise of God and his creation. To him the earth was God's own garden and he believed it was his duty to make the world a better place.

Things had been different when grandfather Schwartz was alive back in the 1860s and the years that followed. Yet he was able to capture the essence of ecology—the sense of the earth as community and what he owed to it. He was a man bound by the economics of his day, but not only that. As a good Jew, he was faithful to both law and customs which formed the foundation of meaning in his life and every part had meaning and meaning was everything.

Grandparents who are professionals, especially in the fields of science and technology, need to be challenged to lead the way into the future. Moving into the future calls for new patterns of existence, new ways of living integrated with the ever-renewing cycles of the natural world. Drawing on personal experience which spans the vast series of changes and on advanced scientific expertise, they are able to envisage with special clarity this new period in society and in the world community.

Grandparents of this present generation have carried out a unique role in the history of the earth. They have intensified the vision that makes survival possible. They have sensitized the world to adjustments that can lessen the damage to the planet and can enhance its benefits for future generations. In moving from an industrial-technological age to an ecological one, grandparents are called to take the lead in sharing their vision of hope with the present generation and with those yet to come.

Grandmother Ida Ruth Miller's five grandchildren have caught her fire of enthusiasm for bringing back all of the native wildflowers that the pioneers found when they settled in Iowa more than 150 years ago. At Living History Farms near Des Moines, Ida planted most of the wildflowers there herself.

Her love and appreciation for her woodland plants began when she was a young girl growing up on her family's farm in southeastern Iowa. There she first came to know such woodland gems as wild geranium, skunk-cabbage, jack-in-the-pulpit, and hepatica. Today her grandchildren are doing the same.

Walking through the woods—affectionately called, "Grandma's Woods"—is not just a chance to see how Grandma carefully nurtures the plants but an opportunity for her grandchildren to learn respect and benevolence for everything in nature, especially what is beautiful and fragile. Ida takes the time to pass on her legacy of love and compassion. According to her, "It doesn't matter if they know the name of each flower. The academic part can come later. What is most important is that we all feel a contentment from being in the woods."

Ida Ruth Miller is a living example for the entire family. Each day she walks through the woods celebrating each new clump of wild blossoms, the reward for the family who join with her twice a year for the planting project. Her daughter, Jane, reports that when she walks with her, she is touched by her sensitivity to every little change, and she herself is caught up in her happiness of being a part of those changes.[14]

Because of her effort and example, hundreds of wildflowers have been reintroduced into the family woods—wildflowers that will awaken each spring for the generations that follow her steps into the woods.

A Lasting Legacy

Personal history inevitably points to those individuals who have had some role in shaping our lives. In many instances, a grandparent's influence predominates over and above that of others. The effect of their presence can be so pervading that, years after their death, the legacy of attitudes toward life, of shared knowledge, or of habits of action continue to live on in us.

Former cabinet member and president of the American Red Cross, Elizabeth Dole, does not hesitate to express her love for her grandmother and pay tribute to her. Mom Cathey, as she called her, was her role model. She lived within two weeks of her hundredth birthday.

On Sunday afternoons she and the other children in the neighborhood were drawn to Mom Cathey's house by the lemonade and cookies. There she would read from her Bible— now one of Elizabeth's favorite possessions.

To Elizabeth, Mom Cathey practiced what she preached and lived her life for others. When her son was killed in an automobile accident, the insurance policy on his life built a hospital wing in a far-off church mission in Pakistan. Anything she could spare went to the ministers at home and the missions abroad. When, in her nineties, it became necessary for her to go to a nursing home, she welcomed the opportunity. She recounts her grandmother saying, "Elizabeth, there might be some people there who don't know the Lord, and I can read the Bible to them."

After the death of her grandmother, Elizabeth found the notes Mom Cathey wrote in the margins of her Bible. She wrote the notes in the middle of the night when she could not sleep. By Psalm 139 she found this notation—"May 22, 1952, 1:00 a.m.—My prayer: Search me, oh God, and know my heart—try me, and know my thoughts. And see if there be any wicked way in me, and lead me in the way everlasting."

Elizabeth cannot remember an unkind word escaping from Mom Cathey in all the years she's known her or an ungracious deed marring her path. "Mom Cathey was an almost perfect role model," reflects Elizabeth who draws from the life of her grandmother strength for her own spiritual journey.

Richard Wayne Dirksen, grandfather of five and father of four, takes seriously the importance of role modeling. As an accomplished composer, conductor, and musician in the nation's capital, he is noted for having one of the most outstanding careers in American music and churchmanship in this century. In 1991, upon his retirement, he was interviewed by his church and spoke about his inspiration for living: "Most important, make of your life a 'Temple not built with hands,' make it your life of giving to others, cathedral-like in dimension, and in authority, in richness, and in loving, an all-embracing example."[15]

When grandparenting can be experienced as growing by giving, not only of mind and heart, but of life itself, then it can become a movement toward the hour when one can say with St. Paul: "As for me, my life is already being poured away as a libation, and the time has come for me to be gone. I have fought the good fight to the end. I have run the race to the finish; I have kept the faith (2 Tm 4:6-7).

Grandparents, as models of aging, plant the seeds for what children can be and how they can become so. They are the signposts of confidence that point the way to the future. From them the young pick up direction on fruitful and fearless aging. They even learn what it means to be a wise grandparent. As an example of graceful and grace-filled aging, grandparents instill in the young the strength to take up the challenge to live to the full. Their very presence inspires this hope.

Tips on Dispelling Age Biases

1. Respect the dignity of the body, even though it ages, by treating it with proper diet and exercise.
2. Keep one's mind alert by intellectual, social, and artistic activities.
3. Keep a human spirit alive by loving faithfully and energetically.
4. Keep a sense of proportion and a sense of humor in the face of diminishments and disappointments.
5. Preserve an inner conviction that through God's love, "Your youth is renewed like the eagle's" (Ps 103:5).
6. Face the possibility of illness and death with faithful acceptance and trust in God.
7. Realize that inner beauty can ever reveal itself more and more fully despite inevitable cosmetic limitations.
8. Don't hesitate to speak to one's grandchildren, gently but frankly, of the limiting situations that every human faces.
9. Exemplify the spirit of Julian of Norwich that, despite the very real evils in this life, "All shall be well and all shall be well and all manner of thing shall be well."

5

GRANDPARENTS AS *SAGES:* ENLIGHTENING THE SPIRIT

While growing up, I often heard my father speak of the "good old days" when he was young. Life was more difficult then than it is now. Belonging to a family of ten meant that everyone had to work harder and make sacrifices and do without the technological conveniences we take for granted. Nevertheless, he still savored the past. He would not want to repeat it, but he did appreciate it: "Things were simpler then, more clear-cut. It was a good time for families."

Today, grandchildren find themselves in the midst of a "communications explosion." The rat race has become a paper chase—and more. The extravagant abundance of television shows, movies, concerts, records, tapes, and compact discs has exceeded in popularity the print media—the hardcovers, paperbacks, magazines, and newspapers. Even so, the publication of the written word and its easy circulation through inexpensive copying dwarfs what had been available when the grandparents of today were children.

Reliance on one's peers as authentic guides in matters of value and wisdom hardly suffices for grandchildren. They find their contemporaries as confused and perplexed as they are, puppets on the strings of fad and fancy. Also, young people depend largely on the television media to transmit and translate for them the latest happenings. But do they really know what life is when the data gets filtered through those in control of the media and censored by the many "politically correct" restrictions placed on those reporting it? Is the public being fed biased expressions or surface impressions without true insight into reality? For many young minds, information itself becomes highly questionable.

Symptoms of this existential malaise are seen in the dramatic increase of drug use, suicides, violence, teenage pregnancies, hate crimes, and educational failures. What is lacking for many young people is a standard of values to enable them to put their actions into a meaningful perspective. They need not only correct information, but also help in assessing the values in their lives. Young people are idealistic. And they cling to these ideals, unless their spirits are numbed by sleaziness and cynicism and a disheartening sense that the world is irrational and indifferent.

All young people have an endless supply of questions, but not just for facts. Questions that merely elicit factual information have been given priority in our society and in our lives. The time has come to begin asking qualitative questions that relate to life's deeper meaning and value. Based on answers to such questions, young people can more easily lead principled lives.

Parents and grandparents should be seriously concerned about the effect of the information glut on the youngsters of the electronic age. How are they going to cope with this overwhelming mass of material: much of it trashy, some of it very good, some of it dehumanizing? How are they going to learn to distinguish between information and disinformation, between information and wisdom? Discernment comes from the experienced and the wise. Age usually is the price we pay to learn discernment. That is why wise grandparents enjoy so crucial a role in teaching their grandchildren to be selective in the intellectual and emotional smorgasbord that the cultural media so seductively present. Children need to understand that selectivity is the key to wisdom, just as wisdom is the door to personal fulfillment. Grandparents can join with them in answering T.S. Eliot's question: "Where is the wisdom we have lost in knowledge?"[1]

Expanding Horizons

Information is necessary but insufficient. Wisdom, even more necessary, is often elusive. Grandparents, like matchmakers can bring young minds and wisdom into an enduring union.

Wisdom sounds as if it belongs in an elitist philosophical enclave. Actually, wisdom dwells also in the common sense world of everyday living. The core of wisdom is order. "It belongs to the wise person to order things," says Aquinas. He spoke not of commands but directives. The wise person starts by bringing direction into his or her own life. Direction requires principles for personal fulfillment. The wise person has discovered the king of judgments and the kind of decisions that make for fulfillment.

Experts in psychology and sociology, after taking a long look at a person's aging process, have concluded that the life journey, or the various stages of life that we experience, should culminate in wisdom. Indeed, life should find not only its culmination but its celebration in wisdom. In growing old, a person should be increasingly able to say, "Aha, so that's how it all fits together!" This coming of age should become a dawning of new light.

What does this wisdom look like to the average observer? At first glance, it resembles the practical intelligence possessed by those who are successful in one or another walk of life. But wisdom goes beyond those narrow confines. Its aim is broader: living a truly good life. It is more than just knowing something; it is deciding flexibly and responsibly. A wise person appreciates the overall patterns that emerge and effectively manifests a mature care, a care which reaches beyond children or work and embraces the whole of God's creation.

Seeking wisdom is not a pursuit of trivia but a quest for

essentials. Wisdom is more than information; it reveals the real meaning and value of life. It answers the eternal questions that throughout human history all peoples have asked about their origin and their end: Where do we come from? What are we here for? Where are we going? These are not questions that only the intellectuals are competent to answer. They are questions that every person asks and tries to answer. Even very young children wonder about these profundities. As they grow older, they become distracted, but as they really grow old, the age-old questions emerge once again. And they try to answer questions that never actually disappeared but surfaced spontaneously in times of heartache, failure, and illness as well as in joyous times of love and creativity and gratitude. Religion, of course, reminds its followers of these deep, personal concerns. Regularly having heard the scripture prompts the mind, when the occasion arises, to attend seriously to these profound issues.

Wisdom, then, is an expanding of human horizons beyond the trivial and merely informative and pleasurable, beyond the limited realms of law and politics, science and medicine, and other laudable pursuits beyond even one's friends and relatives, beyond one's own life. To put it another way, wisdom enables us to grasp the real meaning and value in our lives and our loves, so that with a mind expanded by the length and breadth and depth of wisdom, we can live and love more truly. Ultimately, being wise means being a participator in the wisdom of God, about which we read: "She reaches from end to end mightily and orders all things graciously" (Wis 8:1).

Grandparents, pondering their own lives, can discover an important connection between the bulk of information that bombards us all, and the overarching principles of meaning and value. Owing to this deepening of consciousness, the elderly have been called by Erik Erickson, "the wisdom generation." To appreciate the potential of grandparents who have been truly seasoned through prudent living, we shall try to discover the dimensions of human wisdom.

Wisdom is not something new, nor is it the exclusive possession of the old. Indeed the wisdom of the young Daniel ("My judge is God") is proverbial: Daniel at the trial of Suzanna, at Belshazzar's feast, and in the den of lions. Wisdom is more a question of insight and goodness and responsibility than of age. Nevertheless, experience is necessary, hence the link with aging. Wisdom is not dependent on how much one knows in other areas. Abundance of knowledge is not the test. We all know grandparents who have lived a long life and who now have difficulty in remembering particulars. They are, however, often still valued family counselors. Their assessment of a situation is what is important, not their mastery of the petty details. Alfred, Lord Tennyson reminds us: "Knowledge comes, but wisdom lingers."

Two basic components of the wise are experience and insights. Grandparents have lived long enough to have seen a variety of situations and their sequels. Much they have learned vicariously watching real life drama unfold in lives familiar to them. Much, too, have they had to learn painfully. The blend of observation and involvement feeds into sound judgment. They have learned to assess all the surrounding circumstances and then make a seasoned judgment that best balances the competing probabilities.

Of course, young people have insights into the meaning and value of their experiences. They are perceptive and bright. But young people too easily make snap judgments and leap to conclusions. What everyone needs to do and what younger people often forget or are unable to do is to verify one's preliminary understanding before acting upon it. This task is done through marshalling and weighing the data. Verification is a rechecking of one's understanding so that one can affirm or deny it with certainty. Verification takes time—and experience. Wise judgments are the product of verified insights. Grandparents have had extended opportunities to test and check their understanding of life. Their horizons gradually encompass more and more fundamental meanings and values. Following these emerging patterns, they gradually grow in wisdom through a continuum of successes and failures. They are able to order their actions in reasonable expectation of fulfillment by putting experience to the test of time. Wisdom authenticates ordinary knowledge.

When it comes to one's own life, a person who has been shaped by wisdom may not necessarily remember chapter and verse, but can recall the founding events, the stepping stones, turning points, and hidden dangers. Such a person can discern a common thread woven into the stages of life. In the final years, acknowledging that life is often messy and full of contradictions, one is still able to be resigned toward those things that cannot be changed and yet remain open to new possibilities, and see meaning and value in both. The wise person not only perceives the sound meanings and solid values at the heart of the matter, but also achieves a delicate balancing of equities despite the problematic contingencies of an opaque situation. This kind of wisdom was evident in the grandmother of Andrei Sakharov, one of the great heroes of the twentieth century.

In his *Memoirs*, Sakharov recalls two significant remarks of his paternal grandmother: "The Russian peasant wants to own his land—the Bolsheviks are sure to miscalculate this!" And again, "Still, the Bolsheviks have managed to get things in order; they've strengthened both Russia and their own hold on power. Let's hope things will be easier for ordinary people from now on."[2]

Sakharov's grandmother accepted the new "imperial order" as a source of temporary peace. For her, real "peacetime" meant the era prior to 1914. True peace had not returned since that time. Apparently her greatest influence on Sakharov was that "she anticipated and hoped for a progressive improvement in conditions."[3] It became the destiny of her grandson, Andrei, however, to play a critical role in challenging the repressive Soviet system that eventually led to radical change. Today many credit Sakharov with the changes that have swept not only his own country, but also the countries of Eastern Europe. The grandmother had an "obstinate" conviction that positive change was possible; the grandson helped make that dream a reality. In her wisdom, she has fruitfully expanded his political horizons to encompass a world of freedom and peace.

The Religious Vision

Religion is important in the formation of wise men and women because it gives light and direction. Especially noteworthy is the wisdom literature of the Bible—Proverbs, Ecclesiastes, Sirach, and the Wisdom of Solomon—which has distilled in memorable and poetic statements the diverse aspects of this heavenly wisdom. In Job and the Psalms, this same revelation continues in a more poetic vein. Of course, the wisdom theme permeates the whole Bible, including the historical, legal, and prophetic books. Revealing as it does the ways of God with his creatures, the Bible is a mine of enlightenment and inspiration.

Grandparents, prompted by tragedy or by a need for consolation and encouragement, often turn to the word of God. But sacred scripture does more than give doctrinal and moral principles; it also affords valuable role models, people who have surmounted adversity through their recourse to the grace and the forgiveness of God.

Acts of public worship may introduce one to the biblical heritage. Some will recall that the first time that they really thought about wisdom was when they were preparing for the celebration of their coming of age through confirmation, the Christian sacrament of spiritual maturity. Wisdom has a preeminent place among the other gifts of the Spirit, which are bestowed at that time: understanding, counsel, fortitude, knowledge, piety, and fear of the Lord. Wisdom, complemented by the other intellectual and moral gifts, leads to a savoring of the things of God. Similarly, the young Jewish male celebrates the Jewish ritual of Bar Mitzvah ("son of the commandment"), when he has completed his thirteenth year, thereby reaching the age of responsibility and religious duty. From that time forward, he is called upon to act with wisdom and fidelity. For young Jewish girls there is the Bat Mitzvah ceremony. Both the

Jewish and Christian liturgy leads people back to the revealed notion of wisdom.

Grandparents, in sharing their wisdom with the young, may find encouragement from the fact that the books of sacred scripture were written by the elders of the community. In ancient times, old people held an honored place. They were recognized as citizens worthy of great esteem because of their acquired wisdom. The elders, the senior tribesmen of Israel, were the decision makers in matters of local governance and legal justice. Their memory of rules and customs made them indispensable in deciding lawsuits and judging crimes. This function was manifest in both the Old and the New Testaments as the political matrix of the spiritual. In both spheres, the elders, who were usually grandfathers, predominated. But it was not just their secular expertise that recommended them. Above all, it was their participation in divine wisdom.

For most purposes, the Bible revealed a man's world. But wisdom was personified as female throughout the Wisdom books. We should not, however, overlook the real life, wise women spoken of generally (2 Sam 14:2; 20:16) and some heroic ones mentioned individually like Esther and Judith. Of special import is the role of Miriam, the older sister of Moses and a leader of the early Jewish community: "For I brought you up from the land of Egypt, and delivered you from the prison house, and I sent before you Moses, Aaron, and Miriam" (Mic 6:4).

The role of women in handing on the religious tradition is still alive in Judaism today. Lovella Solar, age sixty-six, a resident of the Hebrew Home of Greater Washington in Rockville, Maryland, was one of five women to become bat-mitzvah (a daughter of the covenant). A candle lighting began the service. Each candle represented a wish made by one of the women.

"This candle is in memory of my grandmother," stated Lovella. "All I learned about Judaism I learned from her. May we now be an inspiration to other generations."[4]

A modern-day counterpart in a leadership role as wise women is Maggie Kuhn, born in 1905 and founder of the "Gray

Panthers," an organization that has done so much in mobilizing the elderly to help their own cause and to assume their responsibility for future generations. Having devoted her life to social reform, both within the Presbyterian church and society at large, her forced retirement at the age of sixty-five launched Maggie further into her campaign for social change. Since that time she has been the recipient of nineteen honorary doctoral degrees, a tribute to her untiring work and outspoken advocacy for the cause of justice.

Maggie has helped people to recognize the importance of reaching out to others. She has worked with many groups, especially those of women who have led very private lives within their immediate families and have never learned how to extend their reach outside that family. Her effort has been to empower such women to make a difference in today's world.

Maggie recognizes the value of welcoming change—originating it and even orchestrating it—and the need to distinguish "good change from evil change." She challenges others to broaden their horizons with the changing times. "We can manage change," she asserts, "and your own history reassures you of this fact. You get a start in self-esteem from your own history because you have already coped with all those things."

Maggie believes that we need values and goals. "Many people retire only to retire from life. What a waste!" she laments. She wants her own life to demonstrate those key values that make the world a better place for all. She describes her life as filling the four roles of mentor, monitor, mediator, and mobilizer. As *mentor*, she acknowledges the necessity for working hand-in-hand with the younger generation, passing on to them the legacy of what she once received from others. As *monitor*, she is watchful of public life, watching the courts, watching City Hall, and watching the media. As *mediator*, she helps to resolve disputes with those holding different points of view. Finally, as *mobilizer*, she organizes and executes, or as she puts it, "gets on with the show."

"I think of myself as a tribal elder," she says. "We are the elders of the tribe," she continues, "and we need to make sure

the tribe survives." Maggie recognizes the need for the grandparent generation to take the lead in passing on the torch of
justice and peace for all. In furthering the values that promote
a flourishing society in a healthy planet, she wants her vision to
be shared by young and old alike.[5]

Linking together wisdom and age, the Bible elaborates the
meaning of wisdom for the people of God. Wisdom is primarily
knowledge about God and his law. Certain salient points
emerge. First of all, wisdom is from God and leads to God.
Wisdom looks at all things in terms of their relationship to
God. Two kinds of subject matter constitute wisdom: the essential, that looks to the way humans and God relate; and the practical, that looks to the way humans deal with one another so
that they do not impede but rather foster their search for God.
So essential wisdom teaches us of God's goodness and power,
his justice and mercy. We learn also of the shortness of life, the
folly of sin, the inevitability of suffering, the benefits of virtue
and fidelity, the need to obey the divine law. Practical wisdom
teaches the proper way to act in the variety of situations that
deal with spouses, children, enemies, friends, rulers, and beg-
gars, the making of loans, almsgiving, boasting, drunkenness,
anger, riches, and poverty.

Above all, the Wisdom books discuss essential wisdom, the
greatest of the gifts of God and the most pressing need and
duty of human beings. Ben Sira says that the only road leading
to a participation in divine wisdom is fear of the Lord. Wisdom
comes only to the one who fears the Lord and does his will. He
calls the fear of the Lord both "the beginning of Wisdom" and
"the fullness of Wisdom." It is not a craven fear, but more a fil-
ial fear, a reverential fear, one that is not incompatible with
trust and love, one that anticipates mercy and forgiveness. Fear
of God acknowledges the supreme dominion of God, his over-
lordship of all. The quest for wisdom and its practical imple-
mentation is a lifetime task: "From your youth, embrace discipline; thus you will gain wisdom with graying hair (Sir 6:18).
This statement prompts grandparents to begin early to incul-

cate the principle of the fear of the Lord in the dearly loved grandchildren.

It bears repeating that this fear of the Lord is not an unpleasant response to a divine superego. It is something that gladdens the heart and that leads to the deepest happiness: "Fear of the Lord is glory and exultation, gladness and a festive crown. Fear of the Lord rejoices the heart, giving gladness and joy and length of days" (Sir 1:11-12). Young people must learn that God is a loving God, not a harsh taskmaker. Loving grandparents have a special role in so characterizing the divine through the example of their own balance of discipline and tenderness.

Dr. Pran Nath Luthra, former executive director of the International Union of Family Life Organizations, shared with me the religious influence that his wise grandfather had in his life. "When I was a boy in India, I would often go for daily walks in the garden with my grandfather. As we walked, grandfather would recite the wise sayings and proverbs from the sacred writings. Later in life whenever I find myself undergoing difficult circumstances, the wise sayings my grandfather recited come to me and I am strengthened." It is interesting how in modern India as in ancient Israel, wise men have taught in maxims and proverbs.

With wisdom one has the strength to transcend the limits of time and space, for wisdom metaphorically bridges the gap between earth and heaven—between the temporal and the eternal. It fashions us with a receptive mode of consciousness that is opened to higher reality. Taking what is obvious to the senses, it seeks beyond for deeper meaning and value. Florida Scott-Maxwell offers us an example of heightening analogy.

Looking back at her life, this eighty-three year old sage described, in *The Measure of My Days*, how it had taken all those years to become herself.[6] She recalls the last months of a pregnancy and how her child seemed to claim all of her body, her strength, her breath, and how she held on wondering if her burden was her enemy, uncertain as to whether even her life was her own. Finally, there emerged in her mind an odd question:

"Is life a pregnancy?" Then came the answer: "That would make death a birth." Throughout life, one is giving birth to oneself; at death one is finally full-born. Being in labor for wisdom terminates in a spiritual rebirth, for now and hereafter.

Wisdom, however, does not stand alone. It is built on a strong foundation—in touch with the past, aware of the present, and accompanied by a concern for the future. This receptivity enables one's inner world to expand to greater and greater possibilities. A wise person is able to let go of the past (not denying it) and to be open to new developments—knowing how to take the best of the past and adapt it to the present, yet always allowing for openness to a glorious future. One then lives with expanding horizons that encompass a future of other people, the planet, and God.

Limit Situations

Religion, as we have seen, since it deals with our ultimate destiny, makes us confront limit situations. These situations, in turn, spawn a multitude of crises which demand wisdom for their solution.

A tragic commentary on the need for true wisdom is seen in a highly publicized family crisis. The actor Marlon Brando's son, Christian Brando, received a ten-year prison sentence for voluntary manslaughter in the shooting death of his half-sister's Tahitian lover. His father's statements at the trial dramatized his bewilderment and pain. Sobbingly, Marlon Brando described himself and his wife as parents who had failed. "His mother [Anna Kushfi] came as close to being a negative person, and as cruel and unhappy a person, as I've ever met. I know I could have done better. But I did the best I could," he sadly stated. A clue to what was at the root of this family tragedy emerged during the trial. When asked to take the traditional oath and swear before God to tell the truth, Brando said: "I will not swear on God, because I do not believe in the conventional God, but I will swear on my children and my grandchildren."

How different it might have been for Marlon Brando—and for these children and grandchildren—if he had realized that there is a God who is not only a higher power but also a loving father and if he had followed the divine precepts more closely.

How do wise grandparents respond to life's crises? By welcoming the fracture in their lives as a window of opportunity for grace to enable them to see what it takes to become serious, sympathetic, and passionate about life. With every jolt of life, grandparents have been faced with the need to make new departures, and each time they are invited to widen their horizons and to touch the deeper currents of hope.

Grandparents who fear the Lord cooperate with destiny. "You that fear the Lord, trust him, and your reward will not be lost" (Sir 2:8). They will strive to live according to God's ways and God's plan for them, and they have confidence in his word. "Trust God and he will help you; make straight your ways and hope in him" (Sir 2:6). Each one has a unique destiny to fulfill a role to live out unlike that of anyone else. Within each of us, there is something that tells us who we are and what we are supposed to be. John Sanford, a Jungian psychologist and priest, says that "something" refers to the destiny which is written in the structure of one's being.

As grandparents age, they begin to confront a compelling need to account for themselves, to determine how their life has fulfilled its potential or destiny. According to Erikson, out of this struggle we fashion our integrity. William Butler Yeats, in a poem with the no-nonsense title, "The Coming of Wisdom With Time," symbolized poignantly the goal of the aging process: "Now I may wither into the truth." This wisdom with wrinkles may seem a high price to pay, but well worth it. For meaninglessness, as Peter Berger and Viktor Frankl insist, is something that human beings cannot accept without despair.

The search for meaning in the face of adversity has been an age-old quest. "Life is subject to age and death. Where is the realm of life in which there is neither age nor death?" These are the words of a man who lived some five centuries before Jesus, a young Indian prince named Siddhartha Gautama who, in coming face-to-face with limit situations, began his search for meaning early in life. Wisdom was his reward.

Siddhartha's father, a king, had made every effort to shield his son from contact with the evils of life. One day, according to legend, the youth came upon an old man, decrepit, broken-toothed, gray haired, crooked and bent of body. The next day he came upon a body racked with disease, lying by the roadside; and on still another day, a rotting corpse. He was told that these are ills that all must face. Motivated by this confrontation with the limits of life, he left his wife and child, his wealth and power, and plunged into the forest in search of an answer.

Siddhartha confronted the sobering truth that human life has drastic limitations, that impermanence and suffering affect everyone. From that time on, he poured his energies into seeking an escape from this dismal fate. After six years of strict self-discipline and profound thought, Siddhartha attained wisdom. While sitting under a Bodhi-Tree and locked in deep concentration, he suddenly became enlightened. Through his transformation, he emerged as the Buddha ("the Awakened One"). He had waked up to the truth. He finally understood how to transcend life's limitations through the purging of inordinate desires which cause all human suffering.

Buddha could not keep this discovery to himself. He set out on a forty-five year mission to show others how to achieve nirvana, or happiness. His teaching bore much fruit: the wisdom of the compassionate Buddha changed the lives of multitudes.

Modern grandparents, in facing limit situations, may also become wise and loving role models. Authentic responses to the fact of fragility are the foundation of wisdom. First of all, grandparents, especially as they grow older, must confront the fears that everyone must face, such as the possibility of financial dependence, feeling unloved and unwanted, finding one's life beset with failings, separation from loved ones, chronic illness and pain, and one's own impending death. By accepting these hard facts about themselves, grandparents move into the light of liberating truth. Freed from self-deception, they are open to profound regeneration.

The next step for them is to act in accordance with that perceived truth by wisely determining to live a virtuous life rather than one of distracting amusements. "God grant me the serenity to accept the things I cannot change; the courage to change the things I can; and the wisdom to know the difference," is the well-known prayer that resides in the heart of wise grandparents. Living this prayer from the inside will bear fruit on the outside, making grandparents wise role models, facing the limits of life with courage and undying hope.

As we have seen, limit situations confront not only the old. The young may meet them early in life, and some are fortunate enough to derive special meaning from their own experience of suffering and death.

Young Nicholas Knowles had always been close to his grandfather who had recently died. Now that it was Christmas, he missed him even more. As he sat playing with his electric train that ran in circles under the tree, he remembered the fun he had had with his grandfather in taking turns being the engineer while controlling the switches. One day Nicholas' mother noticed how sad he was as she entered the room.

Discovering the cause of his low spirits, unusual at this time of year, she called him into her bedroom. Going over to her keepsake box, she retrieved a beautiful gold-chained watch. She explained that it had been his grandfather's watch and that now it was his.

Wide-eyed, Nicholas took the watch and looked at it. As he did, his thoughts were of his grandfather. Everything seemed to stand still. He felt the loving nearness of his grandfather. No words were spoken. There was no need for them.

As Nicholas grew older, the watch became an important symbol for him. Often when he was having a difficult time or was afraid, he would clutch it to himself and imagine his grandfather standing beside him. On certain intimidating occasions such as giving an oral report before a school assembly, he would reach into his pocket and gently rub it, and recall his grandfather's presence. By doing that, he felt the support, comfort, guidance, and wisdom which his grandfather had often given him while he was alive. Nicholas knew that his grandfather had always championed his cause, and he felt he could count on him any time.

Sometime later Nicholas read psychiatrist Viktor Frankl's account in *Man's Search for Meaning* of how, despite their physical separation, he was sustained by the spiritual presence of his wife during his internment in a concentration camp during World War II.[7] One morning as Frankl and a companion trudged along a road, he thought of his wife and pictured her with uncanny acuteness. Suddenly he heard her answer him and smile, and felt her frank encouraging look. For him, her look was more luminous than the sun which was beginning to rise.

After reading the book, Nicholas understood the meaning of his own experience. His grandfather, though he no longer was physically alive in this world, was still capable of influencing him. That gold-chained pocket watch made it easy for him to enjoy consciously that spiritual presence. He realized, too, that he no longer needed to depend upon that symbol to experience the love between his grandfather and himself.

Using the watch was a transitional stage for Nicholas in coming to a deep realization that it is the person and not the symbol that conveys the power of presence. In some way he transcended the barrier between heaven and earth by knowing he had friends in this world and the next. Knowing this truth, he did not fear death. Moreover, Nicholas did not need the watch to realize that there is life and a source of help beyond the grave. He now has the watch in a special place in his drawer and occasionally takes it out and ponders.

To experience the death of a loved one early in life is to look at a limit situation from the outside. Doing so calls for courage. To face one's own impending death, however, is the ultimate challenge. It is a time of deep introspection and self-examination. Mark Moltz had some help when he found himself confronted with such a challenging situation.

Thirty-five year old Mark Moltz was one of two men who survived the crash of their small plane in Sherburne, Vermont. Both managed to leap from the flaming cockpit and cool their burns in the snow, then crawl back into the wreckage for shelter from wind and cold until their rescue twenty hours later. Mark's companion, thirty-nine year old Jerard Healy who was the pilot, related how they talked about the important things—life and love and destiny.

Mark, finding himself in a limit situation, prayed fervently, though he had not prayed in a long time. His life hung in the balance between living and dying. Faced with this contingency, Mark thought of his grandfather who had recently died. The strong ties between the two of them were awakened. As Mark admitted, "I talked to my grandfather. I thought maybe I was going to visit him."[8]

The bond between grandfather and grandson helped Mark to accept the possibility of death without panicking and still to pray with confidence that death might even be eluded. Who can say whether or not he would have otherwise survived?

Caring for Creation

Currently, we are becoming more and more aware of another limit situation. The life systems of this created world are being endangered by the wastefulness and lack of care by human beings. To meet this crisis we need to awaken the fundamental values of life. This kind of response calls for wisdom. Such insight is born of the underlying principles of authentic living. The way grandparents make their decisions that have a bearing on the future manifests this broader vision. The key is in a simple question: "How will this action in the long run affect my grandchildren?" Before buying something that might pollute the environment, before making an unnecessary trip, before doing anything that might leave the earth a less secure, less green place for one's grandchildren to grow up in, that question needs to be asked.

For example, the elders of the Six Nation Iroquois Confederacy built this rule into their Great Law: "In all our deliberation, we must be mindful of the impact of our decisions on the next seven generations." This message of wisdom is depicted by Frederick Frank's sculpture on the grounds of the Cathedral of St. John the Divine in New York City.

Because grandparents share in deciding the kind of earth they will leave their grandchildren, they are in a sense, global trustees. Wise grandparents will take seriously their environmental responsibility toward future generations. Such grandparents will be challenging the direction of our modern-day, consumer frenzy. In the process, they learn of the restorative powers of nature—its cooperative principle, its thrift and artistry, and its compassion—only by discovering these powers present in themselves as microcosms. Every environmental crisis becomes an opportunity to learn what nature is teaching them about life and about themselves.

Taken further, each crisis in their life can be a facing up to one's destiny through a heightening of awareness. "Those who fear the Lord prepare their hearts and humble themselves before him" (Sir 2:17). And as trustees of creation, they will realize that the earth community is our greatest gift and sacred trust which needs to be respected and cared for as the handiwork of God.

Jim Berry takes this message of responsibility for creation to heart. Jim, a burly grandfather in his seventies, an environmentalist and the founder of the Center for the Second Law of Thermodynamics, lives with his wife in a wooded area in Raleigh, North Carolina. His concern about the welfare of planet earth and future generations prompted him to share his insights, wisdom, and vision for a healthy planet in an open letter to his four grandchildren and other young people on the threshold of career choices.

In his letter, Jim talks about the beauty of the earth and its diverse life forms, and also about its destruction. He criticizes the present economic system for encouraging the exploitation of the planet and its resources and for contributing to a consumeristic society based on the accumulation of goods. Such a system, he believes, is responsible for destroying the earth. Jim challenges young people to change the system by making countervailing choices in their careers. He counsels with practical suggestions:

> Your model (for choosing a career) might be someone like Freeman House out in California, spending his life reestablishing the mighty salmon to a prominent role in western ecology. You might study biology with a view of restoring plant and animal life to its proper plane, or repairing wetlands. You could study law and do a lifetime of fighting the battle of the ecologists and the environmentalists in the courtrooms; study politics so as to try to divorce government from it subservience to industry and the military; study journalism and write for the alternative presses; study energy so as to kill off the automobile as the central artifact of American life; study architecture so as to conform our cities to the natural. Or study economics, that's where there is so much to be done. An economic system has got to be developed which is centered on doing work that ought to be done and eliminating work that ought not to be done. Those are some of the careers I would like to see you think about.

Jim Berry has thought long and hard about the things that count most in his life, and has become an active leader in the environmental movement. He does not hesitate, however, to pass on the torch to the younger generations knowing that their future as well as that of the planet's is at stake. Jim is a wise man with vision grounded in common sense.

Profiles in Wisdom

King Solomon, at the beginning of his reign, dreamt that Yahweh appeared to him and told him to ask for whatever he might choose. Solomon requested "a heart to understand how to discern between good and evil" (I Kings 3:9), so that he could govern the people properly. Yahweh, pleased that he asked for this and not for himself, promised him: "I give you a heart wise and shrewd as none before you has had and none will have after" (I Kings 3:12). In addition, he assured him that he would have the riches and glory he did not seek.

Solomon's reign prospered as was promised. He built a temple to Yahweh. He enlarged his empire by high taxes, forced labor, and international trade. Having violated the law by marrying foreign women, he condoned and adopted pagan ways of worship. Indeed, his love for women became such an obsession that he had seven hundred wives of royal rank and three hundred concubines. Though he ruled for forty years, "he did what was displeasing to Yahweh and was not a wholehearted follower of Yahweh as his father David had been" (I Kings 11:6). As a punishment, at his death his kingdom, to which his son Rehoboam had succeeded, was to be divided in two. Rehoboam continued some of the pagan practices of Solomon. He loved many women and had eighteen wives and sixty concubines and became the father of twenty-eight sons and sixty daughters (see 2 Chron 11:1-23).

What precipitated the breakup of the kingdom was Rehoboam's rejection of the wisdom of the elders who counseled his father, Solomon. Rehoboam wanted to continue the high taxes and forced labor. The counselors advised Rehoboam how to speak to Israel: "If you will be a servant to this people today and will serve them, and when you answer them, speak kindly to them, then they will be your servants forever" (12:7). But the young men who had grown up with him advised harsh methods as well as the continuation of the excessive taxation and forced labor. Following their suggestions, Rehoboam threatened Israel saying: "My father made you bear a heavy burden, but I will make it heavier still. My father beat you with ships, but I will beat you with leaded scourges" (12:14). David and Solomon had ruled over both Judah and Israel. Now through the rash and heavy-handed tactics of Rehoboam, only the house of Judah remained loyal to Rehoboam, the grandson of David. This concession was made not for the sake of Solomon, but for the sake of David and Jerusalem.

This historical sequence reveals the precarious stability of wisdom. The wise can become fools. The greater the gift, the greater the responsibility and the greater the fall. A grandfather's greatness may be lost to the grandchild through his father's folly.

Because a life of wisdom is a precarious achievement, it must be buttressed by humor. Even persecuted nations, the Jews, the Irish, the Poles have preserved a sense of the incongruity of life to make suffering bearable. All peoples, all families, all individuals need the saving grace of a sense of humor. A young Pittsburgh Sister of Divine Providence, Dorothy, just twenty-one, lay dying. She was creatively talented in music, languages, and art, as well as being gifted not only with a love of teaching but also with a charismatic and challenging influence on her students. She had vowed her whole life to God. Today, antibiotics would have cured her then fatal kidney infection, but a long life was not to be hers.

Nevertheless, despite the end of her hopes and plans for a life in education, she was completely at peace. With a wisdom beyond her years, she accepted God's will with joy and died confident in his love for her and in the conviction that "God loves a cheerful giver" (2 Cor 9:7). Her younger sister, a member of the same religious community, visited her for the last time, totally distraught at the loss of someone so lovely and so beloved. In words that were hardly a whisper, the dying sister gave her own dear sister a final word of wisdom: "In life," she said, "you always have to have a sense of humor." This simple advice communicated her trust in the providence of God and reflected intimately her profound realization that "gladness of heart is the very life of a person" (Sir 30:22). Her spirit, forever young, has continued, even after these many years, to gladden the hearts of her family.

Some thirty years later, a relative by marriage of that same family was dying of cancer. Conrad Kuhn had raised a family— three children and seven grandchildren—and finally retired. He was a smiley-faced man with a little moustache. He devoted his retirement years to helping others: delivering "meals on wheels," working as a volunteer at his parish church, doing errands for ill and elderly people, taking them to the doctor, and fixing things for them. A fatal habit, acquired when it seemed harmless enough, was cigarette smoking. It lead first to lung cancer and then to brain cancer. He died at the age of seventy-two. But the good humor that made his charitable acts so warmly appreciated by others did not desert him. His mind was clear up to the end. People who came to the hospital room with tears in their eyes, were soon laughing despite their sorrow. Days before his death, when the family was discussing some aspects of the funeral, he broke the tension by a typical observation: "When I do die, and I'm on the way to the cemetery, make sure they take me around the block again. I want my final ride to be a long one." As Saint Teresa of Avila once said, "God save me from gloomy saints." She would have loved Grandpap Kuhn.

The influence of the wise acquires many forms and can have unpredictable and far-reaching outcomes. Recalling his early childhood, it is evident to Norman Pearson the major role his maternal grandmother played in affecting his life.

"Without her my life would have been a mess," he admitted. Norman, now a successful Canadian businessman, and to all who know him, a gracious and dignified older man, is also a grandfather of four and a valued university professor. He realizes that much of his success in life is due to his wise grandmother.

"I have a particularly soft spot," he said, "for my own beloved grandmother—a teacher in the slums of Liverpool when 'gentlewomen,' particularly aristocratic ones, were supposed to do needlework and hunting, and shooting. She spotted very early my love for letters, and that I was left-handed. She taught me to read and write when I was four. When I went to school at five, they were very harsh, forced me to relearn to write right-handed. I started stuttering, botched writing (ink blots everywhere) and had nightmares. In about two days, she walked in and removed me to a more progressive school—and believe me, she was a real heroine-figure for me, and I love her dearly."

Of those accomplished persons familiar to us today, there are some who bear the traits of a particular ancestor. Adlai Stevenson, for example, had many of the markings of his grand-fathers.[9] Listening to his grandfather recount stories of his great-grandfather, Jesse Fell, and his relationship to Abraham Lincoln, had no small effect on the boy. After the death of his close friend one Sunday, Jesse Fell attended a fiery sermon holding Lincoln morally responsible for his own assassination. Among the accusations was that Lincoln had no moral courage to do what his better nature told him was his highest duty in opposing slavery from the very beginning.

Following that event a meeting was held to demand the resignation of the pastor. Jesse Fell, appalled by the attack on his friend, Lincoln, could have joined the crowd. Instead, he submitted a resolution that opposed the demand for resigna-tion, asserted the right of any man to express his views in the church, and reproved the "mob" that had caused the distur-bance in the church on Sunday. As a result, the vote in favor of his position was almost unanimous. Peace was restored.

Adlai had unbounded admiration for his grandfather and saw him to be the kind of man he himself would most like to be; the "best sort of citizen," a man who would be moderate, pacif-ic, and yet an effective leader; a man who would persist patient-ly and stubbornly when principle was involved; a fearless vision-ary who was also shrewd, practical, and useful.

Adlai also possessed certain traits of grandfather Davis, who transmitted much of Adlai's feeling for Jesse Fell to him. Skill for drawing out people, for being a good listener, and for being able to talk wittily on many subjects came from grandfa-ther Davis. Adlai inherited the trait of thriftiness from him. Davis carried a notebook to jot down every expenditure—he practiced and preached thrift at every opportunity.

A similar wise influence affected the painter Jean-Francois Millet (1814-1875). His most famous work, "The Angelus" depicts workers praying reverently in a field at noon. In a letter of 1865 (he was fifty-one) Millet wrote that while executing "The Angelus," he recalled how his grandmother, when hearing the church bells, would stop the children to make them doff their hats and say the prayers for the dead.

Some grandparents may never live to see the results of their actions, though they have a direct bearing on their grandchild. Nor are they able to know how many future generations will be affected because of their decisions. Yet wisdom, as the dramatic events in the last decade of the twentieth century bear witness, has far-reaching results. For example, the end of 1991 marked a turning point in history: the Soviet Union had self-destructed. The principles that shaped that nation's move toward democracy can serve as analogues for understanding wisdom and its implications for the grandparent generation.

What led Mikhail Gorbachev to take that initial giant step in radically challenging traditional Soviet attitudes and thus charting a radical course toward democracy? It is intriguing to speculate that the memory Gorbachev had of the experiences of his grandfathers under political oppression had influenced his move in this direction. Both of his grandfathers had been arrested during the Stalin purges of the 1930's.

Gorbachev's paternal grandfather had merely failed to meet the plan for spring sowing but was subjected to abusive interrogation. From that experience, Gorbachev began to suspect something was terribly wrong with the Soviet system. Added to that was another crushing memory. His maternal grandparents lost three of their six children during the 1930 famine, a period of forced collectivization ordered by Stalin. During the same period, the grandfather of Raisa, Gorbachev's wife, was executed by a firing squad. "All of that," Gorbachev said, "is inside of me."[10]

In the years that followed, Gorbachev would be the key figure dedicated to leading the country through the most difficult stage of the transition from Stalinism and totalitarianism. "If I hadn't come to this decision that everything should be changed, I would have gone on working as my predecessors," Gorbachev said.[11]

Instead, he took office intending to reform the system that caused so much suffering for him, his family, his country, and much of the world. He seems to have surprised himself: he had revolutionized the U.S.S.R.! Gorbachev's principles of *glasnost* and *perostroika* had taken on a life of their own. Although these two words apply to economics, they extend analogously to wisdom. Technically, *glasnost* refers to an opening (of markets by removing biases that constrict trade); *perostroika* has to do with a restructuring (of the Soviet economy). A wise person must act similarly by opening his mind to the truth of reality and restructuring his insights and practices. In so doing he lays the groundwork for possibilities of change.

Moreover, this account suggests that the grandparents themselves may not be the ones who actually bring about needed changes. But they may pass on the inspiration and procedures for change through their attitudes, convictions, and their experiences. Although those values may not be adopted by their own adult children (the second generation), they may well filter down to their grandchildren (the third generation) finally to be reawakened and actualized. From the suffering of Gorbachev's grandparents came the welcome bounty of political wisdom.

The role of the wise in our lives are like living pages of scripture. They make concrete the ideals and the directives that move us to fulfillment. The Wisdom books appeal to us both by argument and examples. Since we have referred to the Wisdom of Ben Sira, we can here profitably note the respect for tradition that this book embodied. Indeed, it does so not only in a traditional, but in a very personal way.

Ben Sira's proper name was Yeshua (Jesus), Son of Eleazar, Son of Sira. The usual procedure would be for the son to take the name of his father, and be called Ben Eleazar. But since the grandfather was more well-known and distinguished, the grandson took his grandfather's name, Ben Sira. But that is only half of the story. Ben Sira's own grandson later translated the Hebrew original (written 180 B.C.) into Greek for the Jews beyond Palestine sometime between 132 B.C. and 117 B.C. This translation found in the Greek Bible proved to be of tremendous importance. The Hebrew original was lost for many centuries until the year 1896. Ben Sira, thus, honored his own grandfather and was honored by his own grandson.

This sense of tradition is reflected in the document itself by its account of the lives of illustrious persons (Sir 44:1-49:16). This form is used in the Wisdom of Solomon and in the Letter to the Hebrews (in the New Testament). Through these examples, readers learned how ancestors live on in their descendants.

> I will now praise those godly people,
> our ancestors, each in his own time. . ..
> Their wealth remains in their families,
> their heritage with their descendants.
> Through God's covenant with them their family endures,
> and their offspring for their sakes;
> For all time their progeny will last,
> their glory will never be blotted out.
> Their bodies are buried in peace,
> but their name lives on and on;
> At gatherings their wisdom is retold,
> and the assembly declares their praises (Sir 44:1; 44:11-15).

Grandparents are more than biological ancestors. They are also intellectual and spiritual forebears. We have seen the grandparent as nurturer, historian, mentor, and model of aging. But the final category, that of grandparent as sage, is the most important of all. It is here that grandparents hand down the greatest spiritual heritage, one that assures their descendants a long-lasting harmony with the world and its creator. In praising illustrious ancestors, human beings recognize a truth essential to personal fulfillment, namely, that wisdom glorifies its children and, in a phrase, grandparents are forever.

Tips on Sharing Wisdom

1. Show young people how the actions and events that have most helped humankind are based on sound values.

2. Point out the principles operating in the lives of wise and successful people, and tell stories illustrating the wisdom of biblical heroes and of wise men and women of today.

3. Dispel the myth that religion and morality take the joy out of life, by showing, despite the inevitability of suffering, the happy and exciting lives of good people.

4. From current biographies and newspaper stories illustrate how people that act wickedly and unwisely ultimately pay dearly for their mistakes.

5. Play games on finding the moral of the story or the event—the ethical bottom line—thereby distinguishing wisdom from mere information, value from mere pleasure.

6. Show that you respect an individual's rights, regardless of their wealth or status, such as the right to property, to a good name, to privacy.

7. Use maxims and folk sayings to make memorable the principles of wisdom, morality, and common sense. Update them to show a continuity of values.

8. In conversation with young people draw on their own innate sense of truth and integrity. Guide young people to consider the consequences of their decisions; for example, their failure to vote.

9. Bring people into an acceptance of limit situations and the attendant sorrows that all must face.

10. Remember always to instill confidence in the wisdom and the goodness of a loving God. Assure them that in the long run good will prevail, so that the young people who are the hope of the future will never lose heart.

11. Strive to communicate a sense of responsibility for planet earth, so that all peoples will become caretakers of creation.

12. Recognize your own personal limitations while being open and adaptable.

13. Finally, be thoughtful and good and religious yourselves, for young people learn wisdom best by seeing it in their elders.

EPILOGUE

Grandparents are forever when they communicate a special quality—love. This love is most obvious in nurturing, but it permeates all the other roles as well. As a nurturer, one interacts intimately affecting the physical, emotional, mental, and spiritual well-being of the grandchild. As an historian, the grandparent shows how love reveals itself through the family story; as a mentor, how love works in the sharing of skills; as a model of aging, how love grows and flourishes even as one grows old; and as a sage, how love brings enlightenment about the fundamental truths of life to be shared with younger generations.

Grandparents have a joyous and fulfilling opportunity for an active life of loving. All of them can transform themselves through the love of their grandchildren, thereby fashioning the heart, retrieving the past, teaching skills, facing the future, and enlightening the spirit.

How to put all these roles together depends on individual grandparents and their special gifts and abilities. But love has a way of engendering an integrated relationship despite the radical differences that most persons manifest. The Bible tells us that "Love is strong as death" (Cant 8:6). The result of this love in action is that the grandparents can live on and on in their grandchildren. They are able to embody the happy truth that grandparents are forever.

NOTES

1. Grandparents as Nurturers: Fashioning the Heart

1. Leo Buscaglia, *Love* (N.Y.: Fawcett, 1982), p. 78.
2. Paul Johnson, *The Intellectuals* (New York: Harper and Row, 1980), p. 21.
3. *Newsweek* (February 17, 1992): 14.
4. Debbie Reynolds and David Patrick Columbia, *Debbie, My Life* (New York: Morrow, 1988).
5. Stanley Chauvin, Jr., "Startling Statistics About Children," *American Bar Association Journal*, February 1990, p.8.
6. Ashley Montague, *Growing Young* (New York: McGraw-Hill, 1983), pp. 136-37.
7. "Filling a Vacuum with Nurturing," *Washington Post*, February 15, 1992, p. B7.
8. "Esteem," *Washington Post*, August 23, 1990, sec. MD., p. D1.
9. "Low Wages: No Justification for Selling Drugs," *Washington Post*, September 9, 1990, p. D7.
10. "Struggling to Find a Way to Teach Values," *Washington Post*, July 9, 1990, p. A5.
11. "Generations United Sets Policy Agenda for Second Session of 102nd Congress," *Generations United*, Winter 1992, p.6.
12. Public Announcement, "John Ray," (Summer, 1990), p.2.
13. David Larsen, "Unplanned Parenthood," *Modern Maturity*, December-January, 1990-1991, pp. 32-36.
14. "The Declining Role of the Black Grandmother," *Washington Post*, June 15, 1989, p. B3.

15. "Grandmother Struggles to Pick Up Where Parents Left Off," *Washington Post*, September 10, 1989, pp. A1, A23.
16. "Plea Saves Soviet Boy in Need of Surgery," *Washington Post*, November 21, 1989, p. B1-B2.
17. "A Grieving Grandmother Spared Prison in Girl's Death," *Washington Post*, February 21, 1990, pp. B1, B4.
18. Ashley Montague, *Growing Young*, p. 132.
19. "The Messenger of Bop," *Washington Post*, October 21, 1990, pp. G1, G2..

2. Grandparents as Family Historians: Retrieving the Past

1. George Bush, "The State Of The Union Address," *Washington Post*, February 1, 1990, p. A8.
2. Joseph E. Persico, *Edward R. Murrow* (N.Y.: McGraw-Hill, 1988, p.22.
3. *New Catholic Encyclopedia*, 1967 ed., s.v. "History," by D. C. Shafer.
4. Ibid., p. 14.
5. Margaret Mead, "Young and Old: A Sharing of Values," in *Growing Together: An Intergenerational Sourcebook*, ed. Karen A. Struntz (Washington, D.C.: AARP, 1985), p.62.
6. Alexis de Tocqueville, *Democracy in America*, trans. George Lawrence, ed. J.P. Mayer (N.Y.: Doubleday, Anchor Books, 1969), p. 508.
7. Robert N. Bellah, et al., *Habits of the Heart* (N.Y.: Harper & Row, 1985).
8. "Giorgio Armani, The King of Informal Elegance," *Washington Times*, January 16, 1990, p. E6.
9. "Russia's Secret Weapon," *Washington Post*, March 29, 1992, p. F1.
10. Erik Erikson, "Reflections on the Last Stage," *The Psychoanalytic Study of the Child* 39 (1984): 164.
11. Ibid., pp. 322-23.
12. Porter McKeever, *Adlai Stevenson His Life and Legacy* (N.Y.: William Morrow & Co. Inc., 1989), p.25.
13. Arthur Kornhaber and Kenneth Woodward, *Grandparents/*

Grandchildren: A Vital Connection (Garden City, Anchor Press/Doubleday, 1981), p. 51.

3. Grandparents as Mentors: Teaching Skills

1. "Grandparents' Stake in Today's Schools," *AARP Bulletin*, October 1991, vol. 32, no. 9, p. 8.
2. Woody Herman and Stuart Troup, *The Woodchopper's Ball* (N.Y.: E.P. Dutton, 1990), p. 11.
3. Joseph Galloway and Patricia A. Avery, "America's Forgotten Resource: Grandparents," *U.S. News & World Report* (April 30, 1984): 76.
4. Richard Bolles, *The Three Boxes of Life: An Introduction to Life/Work Planning* (Berkeley, Calif.: Ten Speed Press, 1978).
5. "Family Ties," *Better Homes and Gardens* (Spring, 1987): 14-15.
6. Bob Kasey founded "Creative Grandparenting, Inc.," 609 Blackgates Road, Wilmington, DE 19803.
7. "Family Ties," *Better Homes and Gardens*, p. 15.
8. Ibid., p. 15.
9. NBC Special "One Day In the White House," February 2, 1990.

4. Grandparents as Models of Aging: Facing the Future

1. "Time to Get Dad Back Into U.S. Families," *U.S.A. Today*, June 14, 1991, p. 10.
2. Brian A. Haggerty, *Out of the House of Slavery* (N.Y.: Paulist Press, 1978), p. 82.
3. Margaret Mead, "Young and Old: A Sharing of Values Through the Arts," in *Growing Together: An Intergenerational Sourcebook*, ed. Karen A. Struntz (Washington, D.C.: AARP, 1985), p. 62.
4. John Kirk, "To Cherish Life," *Parade Magazine*, October 16, 1988, pp. 4-7
5. Chalmers Roberts, *How Did I Get Here So Fast?* (N.Y.: Warner Books, Inc., 1991), p. 71.

6. Ibid., p. 70.
7. See Obituary of Max Lerner, *New York Times*: June 6, 1992, p. 11.
8. "He Makes His Tragedy A Blessing For Others," *Parade Magazine*, May 12, 1990, pp. 4-5.
9. Abraham Joshua Heschel, *I Asked For Wonder*, ed. Samuel H. Dresner (N.Y.: Crossroad, 1991), p. 64.
10. Eric Hoffer, *True Believer*, (N.Y.: Harper & Row, 1951), p. 51.
11. Heschel, p. 55.
12. Charles Fenyvesi, *When the World Was Whole* (N.Y.: Viking Penguin, 1990), p. 18.
13. Ibid., p. 16.
14. "Grandmother's Woods," *Better Homes and Gardens/Grandparents* issue (Spring 1987): 90-91.
15. "Richard Wayne Dirksen," *Cathedral Age* (Summer 1991): 4.

5. Grandparents as Sages: Enlightening the Spirit

1. T.S. Eliot, "The Rock," *Collected Poems* (N.Y.: Harcourt, Brace, 1934), p. 199.
2. Andrei Sakharov, *Memoirs*, trans. Richard Lousie (N.Y.: Alfred A. Knopf, 1990), p. 23.
3. Ibid.
4. "A Grand(mother) Batmitzvah Ceremony," *Senior Beacon*, Washington, D.C., March 1992, p. 18.
5. This section is based on a telephone interview that the author had with Maggie Kuhn on March 21, 1991.
6. Florida Scott-Maxwell, *The Measure of My Days* (N.Y.: Alfred A. Knopf, 1968), p. 76.
7. Viktor Frankl, *Man's Search for Meaning* (Boston: Beacon Press, 1959), p. 68.
8. "Two Survive Vermont Cold After Crash of Small Plane," *Washington Post*, January 23, 1991, p. A5.
9. Porter McKeever, *Adlai Stevenson His Life and Legacy* (N.Y.: Morrow & Co., Inc., 1989), pp. 19-21.
10. *Washington Post*, December 29, 1991, p. C4.
11. *Washington Post*, December 26, 1991, p. A29.